Hurt

The harrowing stories of parents whose
children were sexually abused

JULIA WEBB-HARVEY

lip

First published in 2010 by:

Live It Publishing
27 Old Gloucester Road
London, United Kingdom.
WC1N 3AX
www.liveitpublishing.com

Cover design by Steve Kirkendall.

All enquiries should be addressed to Live It Publishing.

ISBN 978-1-906954-09-3 (pbk)

*To the courage and strength of the parents
who shared their stories.*

*To my husband, Peter, whose unwavering support, love and
faith have accompanied me every step of the way.*

CONTENTS

FOREWORD 1

THE UNSPEAKABLE TRUTHS 3

KELLY'S STORY 21

 My Story 25

 The Lows And Lows 41

 Supporting My Children 54

 Will We Recover? 74

ASTA'S STORY 87

 Our Nightmare 90

 It's Such A Lonely Place 106

 The Road To Recovery 121

LAUREN'S STORY   141

   Lauren: A Woman Groomed   144

   The Years Roll By   174

   Another Reality   187

   Thrown To The Courts   209

   Our Life Is Given Back To Us But What   231
   Remains?

JANE & MATT'S STORY   249

   The Night Our Life Changed   253

   Our World Collapses   264

   Let Down By The System   281

   Struggling On   299

   Finding Hope   318

   Matt's Postscript   337

AFTERWORD   339

WHERE TO GO FOR HELP   345

FOREWORD

I have been involved with Mosac since the early days, long before Mosac became a charity. In that time, I have heard many sad and terrible stories of families torn apart by the sexual abuse of their child. At Mosac, we know we reach a fraction of those families who suffer, and I believe *Hurt* will help many people who cannot find their way to our service, or others like ours.

So many times parents tell us that the sexual abuse of their child is not something that they can talk about at the school gates - so they carry their secrets around with them. They fear they will be blamed by others, even those that know them well, for not preventing the abuse. At Mosac, we often say that parenthood comes with an unwritten job description where guilt is written in. When a child is sexually abused, the guilt can swamp parents so

1

FOREWORD

that they feel that they are drowning in it stopping the process of recovery. The stories you will read about in *Hurt* testify to the burden of guilt that parents carry.

When recovery comes, as it does in time, parents tell us that they are still not able to speak about the sexual abuse of their child - because a parent who has helped their family recover does not want to be recognised for it. They want to protect the identities of their children, and so this veil of silence and secrecy continues. *Hurt* does not promise a happy ending, but a way back to normality. I hope *Hurt* will help parents who are in this horrible situation to see a time when their lives are not so dark, and that families can and do come out the other side.

We are very grateful to Julia for the care and dedication she has shown in turning the idea into the reality of *Hurt* – she has worked tirelessly and often alone. We are so proud of her and want to shout out that *Hurt* is a remarkable achievement, which will enhance lives. We are thrilled that all profits from its sale will come to Mosac.

Linda Randall
Chair of Mosac's Management Committee

THE UNSPEAKABLE
TRUTHS

THE UNSPEAKABLE TRUTHS

Hurt is the book that every one of the contributors searched for, and failed to find when they were living their hell when their child was sexually abused. It is the book I searched for to assist my work as a counsellor working in the area of childhood sexual abuse. There are many books written by adult survivors of childhood sexual abuse, but these do not tell the stories of a non-abusing parent. This was our shared search and has largely been an untold story, until now. There is a resource book available, "Strong Mothers" by Anne Peak and Marion Fletcher, which provides information and strategies to parents dealing with the sexual abuse of a child in their care, but it does not tell the story of survival. In 2008 Terry Philpot published "Understanding Child Abuse: The partners of child sex offenders tell their story", a book on the partners of perpetrators, which took us partly there, but not all the partners' own children were abused. It is also an academic book, with an academic book price tag. There are many deeply academic books on the market, delivering a density of statistics in language that makes them inaccessible for many readers. The contributors who talked about the materials available told me that this kind of book doesn't help them. Someone going through this just wants to know what the stories are - tell me their story, tell me how they manage to get through each day, and please tell me that I am not alone.

Hurt aims to do several things. It aims to sound out a warning to those parents who have never considered the risk to their children from sexual predators. All of the contributors would have placed themselves right here before this horrendous level of hurt happened to their children. It aims to show some pathways along which non-abusing parents have navigated through the carnage that has been left by the sexual abuse of their children. Finally, it aims to provide a friend in the room for anyone suffering alone.

All of us, the contributors and myself, share Mosac as the place that connected us. Mosac is a simply wonderful charity, which seeks to provide support for families trying to cope with the traumas of childhood sexual abuse. It was established in 1992 out of a self-help group; women in Greenwich who came together to support each other because their children were sexually abused. It has grown since then, with local services in London for counselling, advocacy, befriending and play therapy, as well as a national telephone helpline. Full details can be found on the website, www.mosac.org.uk.

THE UNSPEAKABLE TRUTHS

Mosac receives no statutory funding, but is reliant on winning grants and on the generosity of its donors. All of the profits from this book will go straight back to Mosac.

I came to Mosac in 2005, purely by chance, when I was pursuing my counselling qualification. Long after those requirements were met, I remained. The ethos of Mosac speaks to me as a professional, and I am proud to use the collective, 'we'. We believe in the individual and seek to help them build their own resources. We believe that when the non-abusing parent/carer feels healed, then they are more able to help their children recover. We believe the loving support of the non-abusing parent/carer provides the best opportunities for their children.

This isn't meant to be a book about Mosac! It's hard when the contributors want to shout its praise from the rooftops, and therefore I have honoured their requests to be thankful for the lifelines that Mosac has provided.

There are five separate voices in *Hurt*, three mothers telling the stories of their children's abuse, and a couple, mother and father, with different experiences of their daughter's abuse. For each, I met them and let the tape run as they told the stories in their own words. I have tried to capture the individual voices, so that you can hear from them as far as possible. In follow up meetings, they all answered specific questions where I imagined the reader might be curious to know more.

In telling the stories, it became clear to me that I might be useful, sometimes as a kind of narrator, but more so in giving my reactions. I hope that it is helpful in having something to agree or disagree with. I hope you agree. Transitions between the contributors and me are indicated by the following indentation...

It goes without saying, that names have been changed to protect the identities of the contributors and their children, many of whom are still young. I have also changed the locations to try and protect them some more. Each of the contributors retained full editorial rights, that is to say, that they were the first to receive the drafts and decide what they wanted to keep, amend or delete. The process of exact transcribing was a very lengthy one, but I knew that the words captured might not actually convey the right meaning, so the process of editing was very important to me.

This book is written for these brave contributors, and other people like them, going through this horrendous journey. It is not an easy read, but neither was it easy for them to relive their stories. I have already alluded to the shelves full of books by survivors; adults who have survived the most brutal and cruel childhoods. For some of them, their parents or carers were the perpetrators that gave them their hellish childhoods. Those books also make challenging reading. Not all parents or carers of children who suffer abuse are perpetrators. It is hard to believe, but they often really don't know that it is happening. They too are often manipulated by the perpetrator.

Why should that be so hard to believe? Because we don't want to believe that the sexual abuse of children takes place, perhaps? Because we want to believe that parents are able to protect their children? Because we believe that the threats to children are from strangers and not from those who carve a way into the hearts of families? Because we believe that the dangers are from perverts operating in online chat rooms, rather than someone we might trust, or even love?

Each of the contributors to *Hurt* will testify that they never imagined the sexual abuse of their children would be something that they would ever know about, let alone experience. They were not ignorant of sexual abuse after all; it is something we see often enough in the media. They would have advocated that the worries they had were about their child's schooling, taking drugs, walking home alone. Their experiences have been, literally, beyond their worst nightmares.

Statistically speaking, most children suffering sexual abuse do not tell anyone about it. They bury the experience deep within them. I am not about to explore why this might happen, although it is a question worth pondering, perhaps exploring with your own child. Envisage a conversation something like, "do you think you would you be able to tell me if something you didn't like was happening to you?" Even that's hard. How do you express it? It is often true that sexual abuse of children takes place in the wrappings of a loving relationship, where the child doesn't really know it's wrong. You will read about Freddy and also about Philippa; they didn't know it was wrong. There are those children who know it's wrong, but like what is wrapped around it, the 'love'. They put up with the abuse in order to receive what they believe to be love. This is Sophie's story in this book. It is also the story, so brilliantly portrayed, of Whitney in EastEnders[1] in 2008/9. Perhaps this is the closest that many will come to experiencing the systematic grooming and abuse of a child. The storyline was carefully

---

[1] EastEnders is a British television soap opera broadcast on the BBC

researched with NSPCC, and at Mosac, we were given advance notice that the story was to break.

Incidentally, the BBC received over 200 complaints[2] about the paedophile story line in EastEnders, and Ofcom received 90 complaints[3]. I don't understand it. Really I don't. I can only speak as someone with some experience in this field; it was sensitively handled. I was working with a mother at the time who would come in and talk about Bianca (Whitney's on-screen mum), relating herself to this character's experience. Her daughter, abused by her stepfather, also identified with Whitney, and mother and daughter were able to talk about Bianca's and Whitney's ordeal to each other. It gave them a route to discuss their own experience.

Why were there such complaints? Is it really because we don't want to believe the sexual abuse of children takes place? Because it's a family show? Feedback we have at Mosac from clients tells us that it is hard enough to talk about sex education let alone sexual abuse. I know it helped my client at the time, and if it helps only one child speak up and say, "help me, that's happening to me..." then it is worth running. Ofcom[2] agreed

---

[2] Source: Guardian newspaper, Thursday 18 September 2008
[3] Source: article on broadcastnow.co.uk dated 23 February 2009, accessed on 6 November 2009

and upheld the BBC, praising it for handling a "social taboo that is not necessarily comfortable family viewing... it did so within a programme that has a well established reputation for handling such issues and was appropriately scheduled. Ofcom considers that the broadcaster treated the subject matter appropriately and sensitively."

Why are we so shocked by the sexual abuse of children? It is our society's dirty little secret, the social taboo that Ofcom refers to. Statistically[4], most children do not say anything, and for those that do, their parents also bear the weight of the secret. Most of the people that talk to us at Mosac tell us they just cannot tell people. What would you say? They tell us that they are too ashamed; they feel like they are to blame - mostly for not spotting it, but sometimes for bringing the perpetrator into their child's life; and they fear being judged by those around them. I believe it is so misunderstood in our society, because we think we know where the risk from paedophiles comes from, and because we cannot face the truth that most times it happens in our own homes. Until we deal with these two fallacies, then we may never be able to help our children.

---

[4] According to the NSPCC, 72% of sexually abused children do not tell anyone about it at the time. In Cawson, P., Wattam, C., Brooker, S. and Kelly, G. (2000) Child maltreatment in the United Kingdom: a study of the prevalence of child abuse and neglect. London: NSPCC.

THE UNSPEAKABLE TRUTHS

When I was researching and writing *Hurt*, I spoke to many friends and acquaintances about it. I was keen to elicit comments and questions from people with no experience of child sexual abuse, the 'man on the Clapham Omnibus' so to speak, as well as those who had experienced it all too closely. Some merely winced and rapidly changed the subject; clearly not knowing how to respond. Some were surprised and encouraging of "what a very worthy thing to do..." Some were curious, and it has been the questions from these friends and acquaintances that have greatly helped me. My short response would be:

"No, it isn't the stranger in the perv's mac that you need to be worried about, and no it doesn't just happen to poor, working class or benefit class families, and no, they really didn't know it was happening to their child."

Let me try and deal with each of those in turn.

Stranger danger. This is something that each of the contributors mentions, and I can only stress it here. In most cases of childhood sexual abuse, the child knows the perpetrator. According to the NSPCC,[4] of the children surveyed who had reported sexual abuse, only 1% were

---

[4] As before for NSPCC

abused by an adult stranger or someone they had just met. The statistical evidence backs up the experiences of the children in this book - all were sexually abused by people known to them.

Why do we believe otherwise? I believe it's because the evidence that we build up in our minds is based on what's reported in the media. The headline grabbing stories we see in the newspapers about paedophiles. We just look at the grainy photographs and think we might be able to spot trouble coming. Children do get snatched, abused and killed. I am not denying this or expecting parents to stop worrying about the risks, but in most cases it is the sad truth that the paedophiles abusing children are known, and welcomed into the family homes.

Lauren is one such parent, she accepted someone in her home whom she thought was a decent enough bloke, from a good family. She regrets it bitterly to this day. Perhaps you are familiar with the concept of a child being groomed by the child sex offender, but it is often the case that the parent is also groomed. Lauren is incredibly generous in describing her own experience of being manipulated by Rob and, with her support, there is a special chapter turned over to her manipulation. It is compelling and shocking reading, and shows some of the strategies that child sex offenders use to work their way into the lives of families so that children can be targeted for sexual abuse.

I am not an expert in the nature of a paedophile. I have a professional curiosity, and there are some excellent reference materials out there. "Monsters and Men"[5] and "Predators"[6] are two of the best books I have read on the subject. Anna Salter says that she is not an expert on sex offenders, despite the fact that she could *claim* to be one because of a "Ph.D. in psychology from Harvard... given lectures on sex offenders in more than forty states and in ten countries...given keynote addresses at national conferences in four of those countries... made educational films.... written two academic books.... even written mysteries of sex offenders...." (Salter, 2003: p7). She says that the real experts are those that lived with them and suffered because of them.

These books give us insights into the methods and habits of perpetrators, but they don't really explain why some people are sexually attracted to children. After all of her research and experience, Salter says, "the truth is, we don't really know."

---

[5] "Monsters and Men" by Bob Long and DCI Bob McLachlan, 2002, Hodder and Stoughton, London
[6] "Predators Pedophiles, rapists, and other sex offenders" by Anna C. Salter, Ph.D., 2003, Basic Books, New York

THE UNSPEAKABLE TRUTHS

'Why?' is a question that has haunted each of the parents in this book. The unfathomable process that makes a human being act out on children.

Why?

Why?

Why?

It must be torture to have this question roam round and round your head, as the need of the human mind tries to make sense of the experience. I would love to be able to give the answers, but I cannot.

Anna Salter makes a great point about sex offenders, we imagine them to be "monsters and surely we would recognise a monster, wouldn't we?" (Salter, 2003: p5). We'd also be able tell from behaviour. Someone who's nice, kind, gentle, fun, likeable, well they're not going to be a child sex offender. Wrong. Salter reports that even the professionals get this wrong, and cites cases where sexual predators have taken in their assessors only to commit crimes later, crimes that perhaps could have been avoided. She sounds frustrated when she writes, "it seems almost impossible to convince people that private behaviour cannot be predicted from public behaviour." (Salter, 2003: p23). If only we could hold this as a possibility, we might go some way towards protecting our children.

THE UNSPEAKABLE TRUTHS

The sexual abuse of children isn't something that happens because you're poor. I cannot stress this enough. You have to take my word that few of the clients I have worked with have been on low incomes or on benefits. Some have ended up on benefits, but it's been because they have been incapacitated due to the stress of the situation, rather than because they were on benefits to begin with. If I am honest, I think it's a middle-class distortion, because if it's true, then I (middle class person) don't have to worry about it. Read the stories that follow if you are finding that one hard to swallow. I'll let the storytellers convince you.

"How did I not know?" is something that disturbs most of the non-abusing parents; it truly haunts them. All of the contributors thought they knew what was happening to their children in their own homes, and the homes of others, but they did not. You might be reading this thinking you'd know, but would you, really? I think this is one of the hardest things that the non-abusing parents/carers have to deal with, that they didn't know, and at some level, believe they've failed in the protection of their children. Mix these feelings with a dose of judgement from society, 'of course you'd know if it were happening in your home, you should've known....' and you can almost feel the weight of the burden of guilt and shame. This is what eats away at them, but the contributors will tell you that and more.

Society expects parents to look after their children, and when that does not happen, it can be the first to judge. Three of the contributors, Kelly, Lauren and Asta, speak of that fear, and how the fear silenced them, an action in itself upholding the social taboo. I'm not sure I would have been brave enough to do anything differently in their position. I am hopeful that giving a voice to them now may help us, as a society, change.

In reality, it is a difficult thing to discover, because most children don't tell. Of the 72% referred to above, 31% have never told anyone in adulthood. Some of the clients at Mosac are parents discovering that their children were abused 20 or 30 years ago. The pain isn't any less, and being a detective in your own life can be more challenging given the passage of time.

Before handing over to the contributors, I want to add a comment, perhaps an attempt at damage limitation, but I have recounted the contributors' stories as they have told them to me. Some of them express views, frustrations, and questions about the 'system' that is there to investigate the abuse (the police), support the families (social services, the family courts), and prosecute the child sex offenders (the criminal courts). I make some comments, also air some frustrations, but the objective has not been, and is not, to bash the 'system'. The law has to be objective, but the adversarial system of the courts means that trials are a contest between legal teams, often using any means to get the verdict they want. This process means the cost to the families reported here is high. It is not always the case, but court can be a brutal experience.

You will gain so much more insight by reading the truly harrowing stories of the contributors to *Hurt*. There is nothing more I can add to this, so I give you the experts.

Julia Webb-Harvey
West Sussex, UK
March 2010

KELLY'S
STORY

KELLY'S STORY

Kelly lives in London with one of her sons, George. She has a daughter, Susie, who also has a daughter. Kelly has another son, Billy, whose girlfriend has recently given birth to a second child. The effects of childhood sexual abuse have ravaged Kelly's family; something that she never imagined would darken her door. Before the revelation of sexual abuse, Kelly thought she was living an ordinary life, describing her family as 'typical.' Typical in the sense that it was a nuclear family with both parents working and striving to bring up their children in the right way.

If you were to see Kelly on the street, you would not imagine that the most extraordinary things have happened in her life. You'd probably pass her by without noticing her - one of the many faces that you see every day in busy London.

I have spent some time with Kelly now, and there is a warmth in her, a smile, a glint in her eye that revealed itself as I got to know her. Meet her for the first time; you don't see this part of her at all. She admits she is wary of strangers. Who can blame her? If the person you chose to be with, through marriage, for 20 years betrays you, then how can you trust a stranger? Kelly has existed behind a veil, which she erected to keep her and her family safe.

KELLY'S STORY

The first time I met Kelly, she talked to me without my asking her any questions. I imagine she selected the bits from her memories that were important to her for us, you the reader and me, in understanding her story. I think it is important that you hear from her in her own words.

MY STORY

I had what you might describe as an ordinary life. I had an untroubled childhood, in a conventional family. Mum, Dad, four kids. I was the youngest, so I'd get away with a lot. Not that we had a lot, but I'd say it was a happy childhood. I didn't mind going to school, I had a lot of friends, was outgoing, a bit of a tomboy in my early childhood, on account of having two brothers.

I got married young. I'm not sure why now, but I guess I wanted to grow up. Shake that tomboy image. My dad wanted me to be happy, but I don't think he really liked him, Donald, my husband. He didn't want me to marry him at all. I don't remember what my mum said about him, but my sister, Megan, well, she couldn't stand him, and kept on,

"What do you see in him?" she'd ask.

I couldn't really answer her, and she couldn't explain why she didn't like him when I would answer back, "well, what don't you like about him?" I loved him, and wanted to become Mrs Donald Christian.

Over time, we saw less of Megan. Donald didn't like her much, and so we lost touch. It was more hassle than it was worth to keep the family ties strong and, as Donald pointed out, we had our own family to think about. Not long after we were married, Bill was born, then Susie after that, and sometime later, George. It was tough at times, but I'd say we were happy as a family. Both of us worked, it was all about work, so we could go on holidays every now and then. The years turned over pretty quickly really. Nothing dramatic. An ordinary life.

That's not what I see now, of course, looking back. All of that's gone now. It was a charade. A shell of a marriage, and a family that can't have been happy. Do you know you never ever really know someone? I thought I knew Donald, but I didn't. I knew what he told me, but that really didn't amount to much. I didn't know him at all. That's one of the scary things. Do we ever really know anyone?

So, when it all came out, the bubble of life that we lived in beforehand popped. It's like it didn't really exist. It was a kind of ordinary fairy tale. The real story of my family is just awful. It's more than that. It's a living nightmare. My children never had a childhood like I did; he took that away from them. Things happened to them that you wouldn't wish on anybody. And these were my children. I hate him for it. He's written their stories for life. He's changed mine too. This is the type of thing you read about in a newspaper, or see on the news. You think it'll never happen to you. Because you're in a good marriage, and your kids seem happy. You look at the newspaper and think, 'that's awful. How come no one knew? A Mother must know? She must know what goes on in her house. Why didn't the kids say something? They must've known it was wrong. How can you be with someone who does that kind of thing to children?' It makes your stomach turn over to think about it.

And you think, 'it's OK. We're OK as a family. Our marriage is good, it's strong.'

How can it have been a good marriage? It was rotten at the core because of him. I hate him. I wish he would suffer like my kids have done.

I remember being really struck by the image of Kelly reading about the sexual abuse of a child in a newspaper. I imagined her reading it, sitting on a brown sofa, lit by a standard lamp. Donald in another chair, perhaps watching the TV. I imagined Kelly's indignation, the horror of what she was reading about, sharing the views with him that she shared with me. I wondered what Donald might have done. Did a flinch register in him? Did he feel anything? Did he feel guilty or even ashamed? Or did he continue to stare at the screen ahead, not reacting at all?

KELLY'S STORY

In fact, he reacted completely differently. Kelly told me that he went mad, saying it was dirty and disgusting, and that they should lock people like that up and throw away the key, and castrate them to boot.

The bitter irony, of course, was that the story wasn't just something that happened in newspapers. It was happening to Kelly's children, in the house she was in. It didn't resonate with her as she had no idea that it was going on. In this respect, the irony is even greater. As a society, we are quick to judge and make assumptions. *'A mother must know'* is a common view, one that Kelly admits to having herself before her daughter's disclosure, but in reality, it is a damning indictment. If we, as a society, assume that the *'mother must know'*, then we wrap up the mother as being as guilty as the perpetrator himself. Period. How foolish is this?

How does the truth emerge? In many cases, it bursts out, exploding forth when the pressure of keeping it in becomes all too great. That wasn't quite the case for Susie and Kelly, but not unusually, Susie chose to tell someone other than her mother. Susie was 16 when she told someone about the abuse. This is what Kelly recalls about it.

KELLY'S STORY

It all came about after a huge row. At the time I didn't know whether I'd done the right thing, but looking back, with everything else that's unravelled, it was. Susie had gone to stay with a friend of hers on New Year's Eve in 2000, and I'd seen Jackie, the mum, in town.

"Thanks for having Susie stay over the other night, she had a really great time." I said to her.

"When's this?" Jackie replied.

"You know, over the New Year."

"Kel, she wasn't with us that night, sorry love."

I was surprised and a bit confused. Susie isn't normally like that, lying about where she goes. So, when she came back from school, I asked her where she was that night. She just blew up.

"Ask him!" she screamed, pointing at Donald. "You're making me into a liar," she continued at him. He was yelling back, and things were getting out of hand.

"I hate it here. I hate you. I hate him. I hate it here. I'm going."

I tried to talk to her, but she was so upset. I didn't know what to do, but I said to her,

"If you really think you'd be better off out of here, Susie, then go. I'm not going to stop you."

29

KELLY'S STORY

So, she went upstairs, packed a few things and left.

I knew where she'd gone. She'd gone to Jackie's. So I spoke to Jackie on the phone, and she agreed she'd keep an eye on her. I gave her some money for her keep, and hoped that it would all blow over and she would come back. I couldn't work out what was going on, but thought a kind of cooling off might help sort things out. Only a few days turned into a week or so. I'd speak to Jackie, who said that she was all right, quiet, but all right. Then one evening, I'd just come back from work, the phone went and it was Jackie.

"I've got to see you, Kelly, I need to talk to you about something to do with Susie."

"Oh, Jackie, I've just got in from work, and I can't face getting in the car and coming over. Just tell me now."

"I'm not sure it's something I can say on the phone. I'd really like to see you. I can't really make sense of it myself."

"Jackie. Whatever it is, I'll make sense of it. Just tell me and put the phone down if you have to!"

There was a pause on the other end of the line. A deep breath, and then these words, that rattle around me still.

"It's Donald. Susie says he's fiddling with her."

KELLY'S STORY

The phone went dead. I stood there, the tone ringing in my ear. I didn't know what to say. I put the phone down, gently like, turned to Donald, and said to him.

"That was Jackie. Susie said you've been fiddling with her. Have you been fiddling with her?"

He went scarlet; all puffed up and started hollering. All sorts of stuff about Susie being a liar, and a stirrer. I looked at him, and wondered what I should do next. Was it true? Was she lying? Why would she lie about it? Why was he getting so worked up about it? I didn't know what to do, so I called another friend. A kind of wisely figure who'd helped me out on a few things before. She suggested we go to the police. I said to Donald,

"We're going to the police. They can sort this out. They'll find out what's been said, and why she said it."

He didn't want to go, and really resisted, and only reluctantly agreed to go when I'd gone on for so long. So I drove him to the police station. He was really quiet, which unnerved me. As we drew up to the police station, he said,

"You'd better take the keys."

"Whatever for?" I said.

"Well, they're going to lock me away, aren't they?" He was ashen.

"Not if you ain't done anything," I said to him.

KELLY'S STORY

We went in, and talked to the duty sergeant. I explained why we were here. He looked at his computer, and said that there'd been no complaints or allegations against Donald, so there was nothing to answer to. The police officer told us to go home, and ring the child protection team in the morning. So, relieved, we both left.

He changed, like a switch had been flicked over. He was almost cocky. We went back home, and he went to bed. It was getting late by then, but I couldn't rest. There was no way I could try and get to sleep. It couldn't be true. When I thought about Donald, I couldn't believe that Donald would touch his own daughter. The thought repulsed me. Sex hadn't been a problem in our marriage, and I was certain he was satisfied. He wouldn't need to go elsewhere. I knew him. We'd been married for 20 years. Then my thoughts would wander over to Susie, my daughter. She's a good girl. Not a troublemaker at all. She's never created anything like this before. So, why would she lie? She said she hated us, but why would she want to hurt us, destroy us like that? At the same time, I just couldn't believe she'd lie about it.

I didn't know whom to believe. I didn't know what to believe. These thoughts chased each other around like a washing machine stuck on a spin cycle. When morning came, I hadn't gone to bed, I was still at the kitchen table trying to sort it out. I knew I had to see Susie.

I phoned the child protection team to see what they had to say. They said the same as the police – no allegations had been made, so there was nothing to answer to. I was getting nowhere.

That day at work was the longest ever. I knew I could try and find her on her way home from school, so I made up some excuse to my boss, and drove into town. I saw her down the High Street, so I pulled over, and started chatting to her. It was good to see her. She looked OK, and I was thinking about how I missed her. I was about to get back in the car, when I remembered why I was looking for her.

"Susie, I've heard some things about what you've been saying."

"Oh yeah?" she was looking at me.

"That Dad... He's been fiddling with you... Is it true, like?"

"Yes Mum. It is." She went to walk away.

"Susie, love..." I called after her. "I'll help you. You have to say something."

In that moment, looking at her, she was my baby, and with every fibre in my being, I wanted to help her.

KELLY'S STORY

"I've got to go, Mum…" her voice tailed off. I could tell from the wobble of her chin she was trying not to cry.

"Later," she whispered, and turned to go.

I got back in the car and cried, and cried.

I was deeply saddened by the image of Susie and Kelly, both lost in the murky truth of a secret held close for many years. They both seemed so fragile, and forlorn. Both seemed to be breaking apart, and I wondered whether this was the lowest point for them. Was facing the truth the hardest part that Kelly had to experience? Was this the point when the world as she'd known it, caved in? Questions were beginning to form in my mind, which I knew I would be able to ask another time, as there was more that Kelly had to share about how it unravelled.

After a while, Susie tried to come back. I was made up when she said that she wanted to come home. Donald was there, but I was certain that I could protect her from him. She came home after school, and we had tea. Nothing special, just some chicken and rice, and she was quiet.

Edgy. He was quiet too. That was really odd. She went upstairs to her room, and it was a nightmare. I couldn't settle all evening. Every time I heard someone on the stairs, I'd be up like a shot, head around the hall door. Watching. It was awful. I was devastated. I'd so wanted her to come home, and here she was, but we were all on tenterhooks. I went up to take her a cup of tea, and she was just sitting there staring out of the window.

"Mum, this isn't right..." she whispered.

"Oh love..." I didn't know what to say to her. I knew what she was saying, and I wanted her to stay, but I couldn't bear the vigilance it would have taken.

"I think I'll go to Nan's."

That was all that was said. I left her tea on her bedside table, and went to fetch the car keys. Not three hours after she'd arrived, and she was gone. Only this time I'd taken her. I knew why she wanted to do that, and I couldn't blame her. I couldn't stand in her way and ask her to stick around with him.

Susie had been away a few weeks by now, and she was adamant she wasn't coming back home. I understood this, and I was meeting up with her quite regularly for meals. We hadn't really talked about it very much. I don't think either of us knew what to do about it. I was still very muddled about it. It just didn't make sense to me. This one evening, I just had to ask her again.

"So, is it really true, Susie, what you said?"

"Yes Mum, it is." She just looked at me, all calm like.

"You have to go to the police." I said to her.

All this time, I was like a ping-pong ball. When I was with Susie, I believed her. She was so calm and so cold too. Then I'd go back home, and he'd be going berserk, mouthing off, and saying,

"I wouldn't touch that girl. I love her too much to hurt her."

He'd talk to me, and try to convince me he was telling the truth and that she was lying. I'd go back to see Susie, and she'd tell me something else. I didn't know what to believe, and I was so confused.

I don't think that Susie trusted me. I could just tell. And looking back, I can understand that. I mean, I'd listen to her, and then I'd come back with all these other things from her dad. So, I thought to myself, I need to get to the bottom of this, so I set a kind of trap. I told her that he was going to have a lie detector test, and all she said, calm as anything.

"Well, then we'll all know the truth then."

KELLY'S STORY

For Donald, I got to him by talking about all Susie's hifi equipment in her room, suggesting that she was taping him when he was in her room. He went ballistic. Quite a difference in reaction to Susie's calmness. But not only that, when I got back from work the following day, everything had been moved. I mean everything. Even my eldest, Billy, commented on it. It was as if Donald had been looking for something, a tape perhaps. There was one out on the side, by the record player in the front room. It didn't seem like the actions of an innocent man.

Donald was getting desperate, and yelling at me,

"You've got to believe me!"

Whereas Susie was like, "if you don't believe me, Mum, it's up to you."

I was going between one and the other. I didn't know what to believe, or what to do. It seemed to go on and on. He was getting more aggressive. He never actually touched me, but he was intimidating. Really scary.

I'd stopped arguing by then. I couldn't argue any more. I couldn't bear the endless yelling, and tension. It was awful. So he would use my youngest to get at me, would send him in with things to wind me up. Only that didn't work.

Susie eventually made a disclosure, she went to the police, and social services became involved with us. Donald was constantly angry and aggressive. One day I came back from work and it was like going into a war zone. He was going off on one. Social services were due at 4 o'clock, and I'd got home just before then. Then the phone rang and it was social services asking if I could go up there instead on my own.

"Of course I can" I said, and he went mad, as he wasn't invited. So I went up there, and they started asking me about George, my youngest. Did I know that social services had been called to his school that day? No. Did I know that they wanted to speak to George on his own, but Donald wouldn't let them, insisted on him being with him? No. I told them,

"Of course you can speak to George on your own. You have my permission to speak to him."

Then they asked if I'd bashed George. No! Was I sure? Yes! Then could I account for the bruises on his back? No. I didn't know they were there.

Well. Because of all the rows, and with George being used as a go between by Donald, I'd sent him up to Donald's parents for the week. Only he'd come to school covered in bruises on his back, and Donald's parents said it was because I'd beaten him up. I was horrified. I hadn't even seen him all week. His family were closing in, and setting me up with social services. I couldn't believe that it was going on. Why would Donald do this? Why was he trying to get at me? To try and divert attention off himself, that's what I think now, only I couldn't make sense of it then. Needless to say when they spoke with George, he told them it wasn't me, got quite upset about that, but wouldn't say much more about it.

I was getting more confused, and Donald was getting more aggressive. He had pinned me against the wall one evening. I had to make a statement to the police, and he wanted to know what I'd said. I wouldn't tell him. I'd said to the police that I didn't know this man any more, and wasn't sure if I'd ever known him. Billy had to make a statement too, and he was getting at him. It was awful in the house. So I went to the doctor's, to try and get some help. I explained everything to the doctor, and he looked at me and said,

"I don't know what to say to you; what to do with you."

I looked at him. I wanted him to give me some help, some answers.

"Doctor, if you don't know what to do with me, and I don't know what to do, what in the hell am I supposed to do?"

KELLY'S STORY

I was in a terrible state. So the doctor spoke to social services, and then the police. The police were going to question Donald that evening, and had told social services not to go into the house. The police spoke to me and told me not to go in the house – that was stupid as my boys were there, but they really didn't want me to go in. "We don't know what he's capable of" was all they'd say. I'd gone to try and get some help and direction, and I ended up worse. The doctor not knowing what to say, and the police telling me not to go into the house with him. It was just awful.

A month later, the police phoned. Would Donald come up to the police station? He went, and they arrested him and took him away. I thought then we might be able to get back to some kind of normality.

I felt so relieved listening to Kelly, when she said that Donald was arrested. The police were taking Susie seriously, and with Donald behind bars, it might mean that Susie could come back.

THE LOWS AND LOWS

It is hard to imagine anything worse than discovering your daughter has been sexually abused, with the possibility that your other two children, your sons, have also been subjected to abuse. Is it worse that the perpetrator was the man who fathered the children; your husband, the man you chose to spend your life with in marriage?

Kelly's world was turned upside down shortly after the turn of The Millennium, and for three months until Donald was arrested, she was being torn apart, not knowing who to believe. At one level, Susie's claims seemed outrageous, and Donald was very persuasive in trying to have Kelly believe him. Kelly was in turmoil, desperate to make sense of it.

The implications of accepting the truth were monumental. It would affect all areas of her life. The shambles it would make of the marriage; the years of love and support she had given Donald. The fact that she had shared a bed with him, at the same time that he was taking a more deviant sexual pleasure from elsewhere, her own children. The fact that she could look at him and no longer know the man she had spent 20 years with. Was there really a monster in his body, performing sickening acts on their children? Kelly told me that she discovered quite

41

quickly that she was no longer in love with him. It was at the time she had stopped arguing with him, I imagine, battle-weary. Only Donald was not tired of battling and arguing his side, so he had engaged a soldier to act for him. Their son, George. George would come in and ask questions, on behalf of his dad, and one day, Kelly was in the kitchen waiting for the kettle to boil, and George came in.

"Mum. Do you love Dad?" he asked. There was steam clouding up above the work surface, running along the cupboard on the wall. The kettle clicked off. Kelly turned to look at George,

"No, George, I don't."

The fact that she knew clearly that she did not love him was a message to her that she could not easily ignore.

The implications of accepting Susie's truth also raised questions of her as a mother. She questioned her relationship with Susie. She had thought it was a strong one, and yet Susie had not been able to tell her that she was being hurt. She had thought that Susie would tell her anything. In fact, they used to sit together on Susie's bed, looking at her magazines, like *Sugar*, and Susie would read out the problem page and ask her mum to reply. She was more often than not in line with the wisdom spouted on those pages. Kelly now looks back and wonders whether this was a way of asking for help. If it was, Kelly was not able to pick up on the subtlety. I am not certain that anyone would. It's not the sort of thing that you look out for.

Kelly was tortured by the idea that such abuse took place in her own home, and she did not know. "A mother knows what happens in her own house," is what she said to me. She says that if someone had told her this story, her story, she would not have believed that the mother did not know. "Of course she'd have known..." she would have cried in indignation. And yet, Kelly did not know. She has searched deep within herself, wondering if she did know at one level, but did not allow herself to become aware of it. It is a tough question to ask of yourself, and I think Kelly is extremely brave to have dared to ask herself.

Kelly is still not really able to make sense of it. 'How did I not know?' is the question that still haunts her today. In fact, she was so traumatised by it, this unsolvable riddle rotating round and round her head, that when Susie came back home, she took the bold step of asking her daughter.

"Did I know about what was going on, Susie?"

KELLY'S STORY

"No Mum. You didn't know. It never took place when you were here. It was buried. No you didn't know. You couldn't have known."

Kelly had her answer from Susie in the months after it was disclosed, an answer that has not changed with time. And yet Kelly is tortured by the fact that she did not know. Because if she had known, she might have been able to stop it.

In reality, she did act when she knew, as the sexual abuse stopped with the disclosure, but Kelly wished she could have acted sooner. Who wouldn't?

Facing up to the truth of the abuse, and choosing to believe her daughter, you might think would be the lowest point in Kelly's story. It is not. The disclosure of the sexual abuse blew apart the life that this family had. After any explosion, after the smoke and dust has landed, it settles, and things rebalance. With the devastation of sexual abuse, the dust never seems to settle, and there are recurring things to face, to try and cope with, or make sense of.

We know from Kelly that Susie came home when Donald was arrested but it was not a harmonious return for all in the family. Kelly was relieved to have her daughter back where she could see for herself how she was, and not rely on brief updates from caring friends and her mother. It was also difficult because George reacted badly to the return of his sister. He would blame her for their dad being sent away, crying out,

"If you'd kept your mouth shut, we'd be a happy family."

Kelly's son and daughter were at loggerheads. It was neither happy nor harmonious. The dust of the explosion was forever being stirred up.

Donald was on remand at this point in time, and Kelly recalls feeling relieved. She knew where he was, and that he could not get to them. Her energy and effort she was able to direct internally into her family, and try to deal with the tensions that were bubbling up.

Donald, however, was bailed after six weeks. Kelly describes this as the worst period for her. It was different to the turmoil that she had experienced in the months after Susie had disclosed. In Kelly's words "this petrified me", as he knew what her routines were, and therefore when the safety of her children would be exposed. It was a condition of his bail that he did not come to London, but she did not trust him, and had no confidence that he would stick to it. She thought to herself, 'I can't go to work.'

KELLY'S STORY

It was school holidays and Kelly was afraid to leave the house with the children in it. She went back to her doctor and he supported her signing her off work. At least she could live without the stress of the workplace, and worrying about not being there to look after her children. In her mind, she could protect them better when she was around all of the time.

She laughs now when she paints the picture of what it must have looked like. She recalls it being a decent summer, where normally, the windows and the back door would be thrown open to let the air through. But her house was the only one on the street with its windows and doors not only shut, but bolted tight. She would not let George or Susie go out. They had become prisoners in their own house. Moving around together, or not at all. She commented on how strange it must have looked to the neighbours, quite out of character. I presumed by this that she did not tell them what had actually happened, and I was right. She had told them a line about their separation, but not the manner of it.

She laughs now, but she was terrified of what he might come back and do. She describes it as one of the worst summers ever.

KELLY'S STORY

Another of low point for Kelly, which she alludes to in the recollection of her summer from hell, was her loneliness.

"I was a family of one," she told me.

Kelly remembers the crippling isolation that she felt. In the beginning she had no idea where to go for help. Initially, after the disclosure, Kelly told us that she had struggled to know where to go, and had turned to a friend. This part of her story is told previously. But where could Kelly go for support for herself? She felt like she was the only one in the whole world who was dealing with this issue, and had no experience of anything like this, and therefore where she could turn for help. She had no idea that Mosac existed at this time.

It felt important to me to ask where she did find help. I think she found it a hard one to answer, because initially she responded with the opposite, where she was *not* supported. Her friends, it seems, did not want to know, and for some of them, Kelly did not want to burden them. For her children's sake, she wanted their friends' parents to treat them the same, so she deliberately did not tell them. As for the friends that she and Donald had as a couple, he had begun to work on them. She explained that with them, she would look at them and think, 'are you with me, or against me?' Donald was telling them things, things that she had no idea about, and they were slowly drawing away and not wanting to know her. Kelly told me about an incident that happened in the local swimming pool. She had taken the kids swimming and they were mucking about in the pool, and some friends came through 'the bit you splash through', took one look at Kelly and turned around and walked out.

"You can't talk to anyone," Kelly told me, and I was haunted by this thought.

She began to cut herself off from her friends. 'Couple' friends were treating her badly, and she did not know where they fitted into the abuse, if at all. It was easier not to tell anyone. An experience Billy had must have crowned it for Kelly. Billy had confided in his girlfriend at the time, and she told her parents. Her parents stopped the relationship. Kelly recalls feeling that they weren't good enough; weren't safe enough.

With experiences like these, it is not hard to imagine why the story remained within the family as much as possible.

However, within the family, Kelly often felt ostracised by her children. The children had a shared experience, and this bond had an unexpected impact on Kelly. She commented that even now, some years later, when she is trying to be honest and straightforward, they will keep things deep and only tell you when they want you to know. They hold it between themselves, and if one of them gives the eye to the other, then they all shut down. Nothing more will come out. It is like an unspoken pact, leaving Kelly feeling isolated, like a family of one.

Kelly's sister became her shining light. Kelly feels lucky that she became reunited with Megan. She was desperately lonely and wanted someone to talk to and decided to try her sister. Only she had not seen her sister for 12 years. It is another example, to me, of the incredible strength that Kelly has, to drive over to her house, walk up the path, and knock on the door. I can barely imagine what that must have felt like to do. Her heart must have been in her mouth, as she was taking a massive risk in reaching out to her. What if her sister had shut the door as soon as answering it? But Megan looked her up and down, and said,

"What's wrong Kel? You'd better come in."

And so Kelly found her lifeline. She said that if it were not for her sister, she would have sunk. Megan would tell Kelly that she would get through it.

"There is a light at the end of the tunnel. You will be alright, Kelly"

Kelly would reply, "but I can't see it."

Kelly's life was in turmoil, and one of the hardest things to reconcile was that she had been married to Donald for 20 years, but felt that she did not know him at all. During the dealings with the police, before the case went to court, she learned that there was a past to Donald that she did not know, and she was fed up with being told by the police, "can't tell you, Kelly. Data Protection."

When Donald was about to be bailed, Kelly's police officer came around to the house to say that the police wanted her to move out of her house, telling her, "you are really not safe."

Kelly remembers looking at him and saying,

"Why won't you tell me? Don't give me Data Protection! What about our protection?"

Kelly takes up the story.

We had our own house, so it all seemed like a complete joke to me. The council is not going to house me, as I have a house, so what can I do? I was seeing a counsellor at the time through the doctor's surgery, and went to see her about it. She said something completely silly, like, "whatever is best for you, Kelly." Only, I didn't know what was best, as I had no idea why the police were being so adamant that we had to move. Social services had suggested that we go into a council refuge. They would have housed me, Susie, George (being under 11) but not Billy, who was over 18.

"Don't you think our family has been broken enough?" I screamed at them.

That was not the best for me. I would not do it. I refused to break up my family. Where would Billy have gone? It was ridiculous. The police stepped in and supported me. I was rehoused on the day that Donald was released from prison. I only found out why this happened in court, after the verdict was given by the jury.

I was praying that it was not going to be a 'not guilty' because this would mean that they'd thought Susie was lying. It seemed to take forever, and you can't do anything. You are in limbo whilst 12 people are deciding what to believe. Then we were called back in, and the foreman of the jury was asked to stand. I was looking at him, trying to read what he was about to say. And then it came:

Guilty. Guilty. Guilty

On all three counts. Guilty! I was so relieved. Susie was believed. But then what happened? Our barrister wanted other cases to be fetched, but that wasn't allowed. Then I heard his previous. I went completely numb. 'What?' I thought. I remember looking at him and wanting to smash his face on the glass panel around him. I had to get out, as I wanted to shout and scream at him. I wanted to hurt him for what he had done before. Rape and Attempted Murder. The police were right. No wonder we hadn't been safe. I didn't know him at all.

On that day in court, Donald was given four weeks to 'sort his life out', and return for sentencing after this period. Susie never had that; four weeks. Her life is ruined.

It seems derisory, and insulting. I asked Kelly if it was worth it.

No. Not really. We went over it all again after the verdict, as we did an impact statement[7]. Bringing it all up again, when you think that the time in court is going to be the end. It was a stupid sentence at the end of it all, and the

---

[7] An impact statement, or victim personal statement to give it the correct title, adds to the information already given to the police. It gives the victim a chance to tell the police about any support they might need and how the crime has affected them; physically, emotionally or financially.

judge wouldn't allow the impact statements to be considered. Donald was given a sentence of 18 months, which was reduced for the time that he had spent on remand. In reality it meant that he spent nine months in prison.

The consequences of this silly sentence, this is one of the lingering lows. He did his nine months, and according to Victim Support, in the time he was in prison he didn't do anything, as he wasn't having any treatment. As far as he was concerned he hadn't done anything wrong. So he's come out, and probably not learnt anything. Who's to say he's not hurting someone else? I wouldn't trust him one bit. So he's doing whatever. He can move on. Carry on with someone else. Delete the past; rewrite it, as he did with me.

It is worse than a bereavement. If he had died naturally, there would be good memories. I'd have support on both sides of the family. But here, that's gone. There must've been good times, but that's been overridden. They've gone. The children don't want to say anything about him. I can't say anything good about him, and I don't want to say anything bad to the kids. So I'm just in limbo. There is no closure. Just shreds of everything.

SUPPORTING MY CHILDREN

Kelly's main focus after the disclosure was to protect and support her children. This became the most important thing she did. It took all of her emotional and physical strength. She was unable to work, for fear of not being there for them. The complete focus on her children is an understandable shift in the way she chose to live. It was almost as if her needs were no longer important. Kelly was desperate to make sure that they would not be hurt again.

When Kelly looks back, she is disturbed by how confused she was when Susie disclosed that Donald had been fiddling with her. She said to me that you imagine you'd be so strong, so sure, and that if anyone were abusing your child, you'd be certain that you'd want to kill him or her. In reality, it was not like that at all for Kelly in those early weeks, months even. She has examined her life in painstaking detail, trying to work out whether she did *really* know what was going on. She cannot find any clues.

The truth is that Donald had perfected the art of silencing her children. He was effective in this for a number of years, since the abuse of Susie went on for an unknown length of time. In Susie's case, only she and Donald know how long. Susie would only say that it took place from when she was 13, but the medical experts said that from the damage to her internally, she was abused for 'many many years.'

To be silenced for such a long time is almost unthinkable. I asked Kelly how she thought Donald had silenced them for so long.

I think it was fear. That was at the root of it, for whatever their dad was saying to them. It was fear, because they are all still frightened of him today. In truth, I'm not really sure what was said, because they can still clam up about it. I only know bits of what they tell me even today. George told me that his dad would threaten him, by saying, "you won't see your mum anymore, as they'll take you away..." or, "if you tell anyone, I'm going to have to kill you...." or, "if you tell anyone, I'm going to have to kill your mum, or Susie..."

I really want to know how he managed to get away with it for so long. Why didn't they just tell me, and know that I would protect them? I wonder if they'd told me earlier, whether I would have done something. That's what you believe. But would I? I went through the turmoil of whom to believe at the time, so who can say that it would be any different if they'd told me earlier. Deep, deep down

KELLY'S STORY

I believed Susie, but that took a while to get to the surface, because he was confusing me. Lying to me, tricking me. He was very cunning and devious twisting everything around. Trying to control what I thought. But he didn't succeed in the end. I believed my daughter.

There must have been threads of stories around the time that Susie was out of the home, with Susie saying one thing, and Donald another. Unravelling who said what, let alone trying to gauge reactions must have been a complete tangle. Kelly admits to setting traps in order to uncover the truth, so we know that there were layers of mind games going on. It seems that Susie was the only one stoically holding to her truth.

In coming to accept the awful truth that Susie had been sexually abused, Kelly's efforts became focussed on protecting her children. Kelly explained that Donald had lost his rights to the title as a 'father' in her eyes, even though she accepted that he was the person that fathered her children. How could she keep him from her children? We know that she felt safest when Donald was arrested and placed on remand; physically he was not a threat, but this was only part of the story. I imagined that this would have provided some release from the grip he had on them all. Indeed Kelly has told us that this was an easier time, because the physical threat of him appearing was removed. However Donald was pursuing contact from his prison cell, with a disturbing impact on her youngest, George in particular.

Kelly recalls how she had to be vigilant to all forms of contact with the children, and how she got into an argument with social services, who initially seemed to be trying to take the middle ground with regards to their dad.

Donald initially wanted to send them presents, but I refused. The giving of gifts, mostly sweets, was part of his way of silencing them during the abuse, and I had no idea how that would affect them. So, we would communicate that back to him through the social worker, and then the social worker would say,

"What about presents from the grandparents?"

No. It would just be the same, like they would be doing it for him.

One day the social worker was there, and made some comment like,

"Oh your dad is sending you his love."

I was not best pleased to hear that, but it was out. When he left, George flipped.

"You're not letting Dad back" he screamed.

He was really hard to console, and reassure. This must've really chewed at him, because he played up after then. After school the next day he went up on the shed roof with a knife. It had really disturbed him - all because of this message that the social worker had passed on. When I saw the social worker, I said to him,

"Look what you've done now."

I laid it down to them. No contact. None whatsoever. The social worker, he was apologetic. He said that he hadn't realised what he was joining in with; passing on messages from Donald was like the abuse still happening.

It felt like I was fighting everyone to keep Donald out. He even tried to get a social worker to get me to work on getting the marriage back together. How stupid does that sound? They said that couples have reconciled for less. But they have this idealised view of how things should be at times.

KELLY'S STORY

It may seem ridiculous that the social workers seem to be working against the interests of Kelly, the mother. From the cases we hear at Mosac, unfortunately some do not understand the psychology of a perpetrator, let alone the effect on the child, but as well-meaning people, they are trying to ensure that there is fairness and that a father's rights are honoured. In Kelly's case, the impact of the well-meaning social worker were perhaps minimised, but why should it take the action of a young boy taking to the roof of a school shed, with a knife, before Kelly's concerns were listened to and instigated?

The law is another matter. There are protocols, procedures and processes that must be followed. There is not much room in the legal system to stray from these, and at times it seemed to me that the needs of the mother, Kelly, and her children were secondary. The aim of going to court is to seek justice, to see the perpetrator found guilty of his crimes and sentenced accordingly. The courts are objective, and deal in evidence, and the jury is asked to make a judgment based solely on the evidence that they hear. The actions within the legal system are all about preserving the evidence in order to achieve the aim of prosecution.

Kelly and her children were all witnesses in Donald's trial. It is almost as if they stopped being the victims, because their function became to deliver evidence. As such, in law, it is vital that the witnesses do not collude, or a led. I was shocked at their treatment as human beings who had suffered greatly, because in court, they had to operate at an objective level. Kelly told me about their experience.

When it came to the court, the time when it actually came, it was terrifying. Sure, Witness Protection people had taken us round, but it was an empty room, not a working court. I had never been in court before, so I had no idea what to expect, but it was the most frightening thing.

I wasn't allowed to sit with them, the children, during the proceedings in case we talked about the court case. It was less risky to the case that we had no contact during the court sessions. I wasn't even allowed in the courtroom when Susie was giving evidence. We were all witnesses, you see, so I didn't hear her evidence. Billy, similarly. He was a witness and he wasn't allowed in. So we had to wait in this family room. We only talked about it when it was all done; I only learned some things about the trial much later.

KELLY'S STORY

Susie, she found it incredibly hard. She was 17 at the time, and she had to go onto the stand, no video link for her. He was standing in her line of sight. He would try and stare her out. She was terrified. I didn't like the idea of him being so close to her. She was petrified as his family were in the gallery. It was like she was on trial. She didn't like their wigs. The judge was good in that he could see what was going on, and made him sit out of sight, but to be in that position; it was shocking. And their barrister was calling her all sorts of names, and asking her to answer yes or no, but there isn't always only a yes or no. She had it really tough.

You are unable to support your children. The law just won't allow you to. You can't go near them. She came out of the courtroom, into this waiting room, in a terrible state. Your natural reaction is to go over and hold her and comfort her, but you can't. I was not allowed to. I had to sit there opposite her, watching, as my daughter broke down. I couldn't talk to her in the week about anything to do with the proceedings. It was like being in a bubble. Susie, she isolated herself, presumably because she was told she had to. She didn't stay at home even; she went to her nan's. I couldn't reach her at all. It was horrendous.

Then you come to give evidence. And it is like you are on trial only you haven't done anything wrong. You know you are telling the truth, and you know that he will be lying to worm his way out of it. You are desperate to be believed, and terrified of mucking it all up in the evidence you give. It was the hardest thing I've done. My stomach was in knots. I didn't know what to expect, and what they might hurl at me.

When the questioning starts, you can't answer in the 'yes' or 'no' that they want. It isn't always like that; black or white, so you have to give the closest you can, and hope that it's helpful.

I wanted to hear what he had to say, and as I had spoken, I could go into the courtroom to hear it. I wanted to hear him apologise. But he wouldn't do that. The things that he was saying were rubbish – just utter rubbish. And you have to sit there quietly and listen to it. It was awful.

And then it's over, all that waiting, and it's over, but there isn't any relief, because then you're thinking about it. Did I tell them right? Did I get it right or wrong? What do the jury think about me? What does the barrister think of what I said? Did they believe the rubbish that he was saying? Was Susie a good witness, whatever that means. And still Susie is quiet and withdrawn. It was like it was happening all over again; only she had to describe it in great detail to a public court.

KELLY'S STORY

The jury are out and they seem to be going on and on. So you're wondering if it's a good sign or not. I have no idea. Then the jury came back, and wanted to ask more questions, but the judge wouldn't allow that and said that he would take a 10/2 majority. At this point, you start going even more loopy, trying to work out if it is good or normal.

I was praying that it was guilty, as I was desperate that Susie was believed. Guilty. It was an amazing moment. But short-lived, as things started unravelling. I couldn't believe the previous that I was hearing about. Some of the jury were crying. And you look at them and wonder why. Did you vote for or against him? Are you crying for the crime that has been committed, perhaps because you chose not to believe Susie, or because it suddenly seems so much worse because of the monster he actually is? I was so angry with him.

So he's been found guilty, but it doesn't actually mean very much. I was glad for Susie, and just so relieved that we had the verdict we wanted. But I was really drained by it all. Then the judge said that he could have four weeks to sort his life out, and come back for sentencing. I couldn't believe I was hearing it right. Found guilty of sexually abusing my daughter, and then released. We had thought he would be locked away, and there he was, being turned out on to the streets. It was a very sick joke. I felt like I hadn't protected Susie at all. The courts really let us down. But what can you do? You are utterly powerless once it gets into full swing.

I was very disturbed by the harrowing description of what it is like to be actually at the heart of the court's process. Like many people, until I did Jury Service my experience was probably seeing TV dramas of court scenes. This gives you no real sense of the human cost, or the extent to which you really have to hand yourself over to the formality and rigour of the courts. I am struck by how much you have to believe it is the right thing to do in order to go through the pain of the process. You have to convince a jury of your story, through the questioning and biases of the barristers, and then it remains the judge's decision as to sentencing.

In sentencing, this is where I felt powerless again. There is a guilty verdict on all counts; some of the jury is in tears. Your daughter is broken, and then she withdraws during the trial. You are waiting for the judge to send him away, so that you can begin to feel safe, again. The judge gives him time to sort things out. Another month goes by and you return for sentencing. Donald was given a completely stupid sentence. It meant he was released after serving only nine months.

The awful thing is that, ultimately Susie said it was not worth being pulled through the court for the prosecution of her dad. Not worth the fear, the anxiety and trauma of the whole thing. We had begun the prosecution believing that it was the right thing to do; that Donald should be tried for his crimes, and face the law of the land.

Kelly is not certain that she would recommend pursuing a trial in criminal court either. At one point, Billy talked about making a statement about his abuse, and George had said that he would make one if Billy wanted to press charges. Susie begged her mum not to let Billy go through it, but Kelly maintains it is up to him. I think Kelly was in some ways relieved he hasn't wanted to take it forward. Kelly felt unable to defend her children from the legal system, despite having a good barrister, a great policeman and a friendly judge. Why would you want to do that again?

The legal system was unable to give satisfaction to the Christians, and in fact had perhaps caused more traumas. It is not uncommon to have the experience of being 're-abused' in the process of the trial, as the experience is being relived.

Kelly was able to make some difference in protecting her children from some of the tangible threats, for example in being firm with social services, but in others it was more difficult. She was unable to prevent the hurt of the emotional damage that Donald had inflicted on his children. Supporting them emotionally was perhaps the hardest thing that Kelly has had to deal with, and still does. She talked about the struggle in trying to support her children, and the effect it had on her.

Each of my children handled it differently. This isn't surprising at one level, because they're all different people, so they deal with things in different ways. I tried to respond differently to each of them, to try and meet them, but it was really hard. My counsellor had told me that I shouldn't show any reaction – not to be shocked, angry, whatever. That was tough. I guess that's because you don't want them to think that you can't handle what they're saying. Like you're the strong one, and if I were to rant about something, then they mightn't feel that they wanted to burden me. I don't know. It was almost impossible at times, but I really tried to absorb it all for them. It's awfully hard. Kids shouldn't tell you anything like that, about what happened to them. And you have to just soak it up. Hold on to everything. I marvel at myself looking back. Why am I not a complete nutcase? I have no idea where I got the strength. I just knew I had to be strong for my kids at a time when they needed someone to be rock solid. I did a lot of it on my own too. I didn't rate the counsellor; what she was telling me to do, so I saw her only a couple of times. I didn't have the strength to try anyone else.

George went through a bit of a guilt complex at one point. He was really angry with Susie at first for telling about the abuse, and sending his dad away, but then he went the other way. He was present when some of the abuse took place, and he felt he should've protected her. What can that be like to carry around with you?

At the same time, I didn't know where my place was, how I fitted into the three of them. We would be sitting around a table, and one would start talking, and another would shake their head, and that was it. The pact closed in. So, the telling was very much on their own terms, which is fair enough, but it leaves you with so many questions. In the beginning I didn't know where to go with them. You're stuck in this place of being deeply affected and disturbed by what they tell you, when they do, and wanting to fill the gaps. It did my head in, trying to work out what I didn't know.

I never knew he had hit them. That really got to me. He would chase the little one up the stairs with a coat hanger. I never saw any of that. Where were the bruises? When they're over ten, you don't bath them anymore, so you don't really see them. George told me his dad would pinch his private parts.... it's just horrific to think that it was actually going on. I didn't know.

Do you know, I used to think that I had a really good relationship with Susie, that she'd tell me anything. But I know that isn't true, because of what she held for so long. So then you begin to question what the relationship really is like. Does she trust me, because I was so torn when it all came out, and do I trust her because she was so good at hiding the sexual abuse from me? It can drive you mad, if you let it.

KELLY'S STORY

Each of them had an experience of counselling, although at different times. Ironically Susie was seeing a counsellor from the age of eleven or twelve because she was "Miss Never Well" and the professionals had thought her constant illnesses were psychosomatic. It was in fact the abuse. We know Susie only disclosed when she was 16, some years into her counselling relationship, at a time when she was ready to. Sadly, at the age of 18 she became ineligible to continue counselling in this service, through CAMHS[8]. Susie had to leave by the time she was 19, which she was devastated about. Now she is not interested in seeing anyone other than the male counsellor that she trusted for some five or so years.

Susie was worried about George at the time of the incident with the knife on the shed roof. Because she talked to her counsellor about it, Kelly was approached to see if George would benefit from counselling support. He was therefore also seen by the same service from the age of ten, and still is. He also took his time to disclose the abuse that happened to him. Billy has sought counselling through his work as a policeman, and has embarked on counselling training himself. Kelly believes that each of

---

[8] CAMHS, (Child and Adolescence Mental Health Service) sits within the National Health Service in the UK. Its purpose is to help and treat children and young people with emotional, behavioural and mental health difficulties.

her children has benefited from counselling, but that it has been a long journey with each of them going at it at their own pace. She describes it as a 'long road.'

When I listened to Kelly talking about the emotional fallout, it is hard to imagine how they managed to stay sane and together. I know at times Kelly felt extremely isolated, and that she was being excluded from the pact that the three of them had. I also knew that each of them would pull differently at her, and I wondered what it was like at times, knowing which of her children to support when they all wanted something different.

It's really hard, almost impossible. Because fundamentally, you can understand all of it. Understand each of them, and why they are as they are. You handle them differently as children when you're trying to discipline them, and therefore it's going to be the same in dealing with all of this. For example, if Susie was naughty, I'd take her books or magazines off her, but that wouldn't work with George, who I'd have to stop going out to play. And so it was here, trying to balance each of them, and understand each of them.

KELLY'S STORY

Susie would not mention Donald, or touch anything that had belonged to him. It was like she skirted around him. For Billy, Dad was dead. That was it. He was gone, beyond gone. Then George was all muddled up, but then he was much younger. He would ask questions. I remember him asking Susie one day,

"Do you love Dad?" I held my breath because I thought it would all kick off, but she surprised me, by answering him,

"I love him because he's my dad, but I don't love him for what he did."

It's heart breaking. She must've been so torn up about it. There was so much underneath the surface that didn't want to acknowledge him, and yet, at some level she still loved him.

I was struck by the complexity of what was being experienced by each of them, Kelly included, within their home. It felt very tangled to me. Just as I was beginning to grasp what was going on for all of them, Kelly then went on to talk more about George. For George, there was this deeply complex issue about what love was. We know he had asked his sister what she felt about loving her dad, and

71

KELLY'S STORY

I can only imagine it was because he was trying to make sense of what he was feeling.

George one day said that his dad couldn't have loved him, because he didn't do any of those things – the abuse - to him. Only, in time, he revealed he had. At least, he would say things, and then later say that it had been a lie. It was like he couldn't decide what was true. The counsellor said it was probably because he didn't want to face it, so it would come out, and then get snatched back. He would also ask,

"Did Dad really love me, Mum?"

I would always say that he must have loved you, but that it was in an inappropriate way. What else could I say? It wasn't love as I knew it, but George wanted to believe that he was loved. I couldn't deny him that.

George would also accuse me of not loving him enough. I didn't love him because I did not love him the same way as his dad did. I would just tell him that his dad's way of love was wrong, and that I did love him.

KELLY'S STORY

I really understand it when Kelly says that the ones with the life sentence are those left behind after the abuser has gone. The physicality of the sexual abuse stopped for each of the children, when Susie's disclosure was heard. However, the consequences are long lasting. They each had to adjust to the reality of what had been going on in secret in the family home. Each of them needing different things. At times Kelly said that it was all tension and bickering, and at others, they seemed to be pulling together. But how long do they carry on being affected? When the trial is over? A year later? Perhaps five years later you would imagine that it is finally behind you. This is what I was intrigued by, and what I explore with Kelly in her final chapter.

WILL WE RECOVER?

In my work in this area, supporting the parents of children who have been sexually abused, many families I meet want to focus on doing something to try and correct the wrongs that have been done to their own. Thus, energies are focussed on protecting their children from contact with the abuser (if the abuser has not been criminally charged and therefore subject to the protection that the law provides), or on a successful prosecution. Safety and justice are battles that the parent/carer becomes embroiled in. This can take a long time. For some, even years after the initial disclosure.

When the judge has passed sentence and the perpetrator has been locked away for however long imagine what happens next? Does the family just click back to 'normal'? Children go back to school. Parents return to work.

For many families, the relief of a 'guilty' verdict is short lived. For some, it almost comes as an anti-climax. If you have carried the burden of the story alone, then whom can you share it with? Do you want to share your experience with the woman you used to go to yoga with every Tuesday? What to say to your neighbours, whom you may have a passing acquaintance with? Many try and return quietly back to their lives. They are as silent in victory, as they have been in the pursuit of justice.

In Kelly's case, the impact of hearing the "guilty – guilty – guilty" from the foreman of the jury was short lived, as Donald's 'previous' was revealed. Even in sentencing, Kelly and her family felt little satisfaction. I have learned not to be surprised at relatively short sentences. However, I was not prepared to hear how Donald had spent his time, or at least how Kelly heard about it.

I don't know what to think when I think about him being released. He denied it all the way through, and from what I know of him, he thought he never did anything wrong. He can't have learned anything from being inside. Victim Support told me that when he was inside, he wasn't having any treatment. So, he's come out, he's learnt nothing. Not been asked to look at anything he's done. Who's to say that he's not hurting someone else? I don't trust him. He didn't tell me about his violent past when we were together, so is this another chapter that is just wiped out for him? It really scares me at times. What he might be doing.

KELLY'S STORY

Sure, we don't know that Donald is doing anything. Kelly's family have no contact with him; they don't want to. But the reality is that Kelly is disturbed by it, and it still lives with her. I can understand why, and why it would get to her. It would me.

Kelly imagines that Donald is getting on with his life as if nothing has happened. Experience tells her it is what he is likely to be doing, with his family complicit in keeping the truth from anyone who becomes involved with him. As they did with Kelly, in fact, when she and Donald first got together.

For Kelly, life cannot quite move past the sexual abuse. I am now interested in how it still affects them, and Kelly surprises me with the extent by which they can still be affected.

The youngest is scared of going to see any doctor still. If there's anything wrong, you can't exactly say, "let me have a look at it and decide." He's now 16, and should be in charge of his own body. He is also terrified of the dentist. He doesn't like anything being put in his mouth. The dentist is really good now, explains everything very carefully, and doesn't make any sudden movements or actions. I had to explain to him way back, when it all came out, what had happened to him. Another person involved in your story. All so that George can have his teeth checked over. If he didn't have to go, I don't think he would. He was worried what his dad may have given him, in terms of sexually transmitted diseases. George told me that his dad had many girlfriends. I knew there was one. He was a delivery driver, and would often have to make long trips. Only, apparently, they were often just lies to cover going to see someone here or there. George asked me why I put up with it. I didn't know. I just didn't know. So, then, I'm wondering what Donald's given me. Perhaps my son has a point.

Billy wanted an HIV test. That was kind of shocking at the time. He just said,

"You don't know what Dad may have done or given us."

So, he went through that, and we waited for the results. Waited and waited. All clear. That was something to be pleased about. How mad does that sound? Pleased that his dad hadn't given him HIV?

Billy has got problems with the doctor too. He had to see a consultant a while back, and he refused to let him examine him. Just refused. We knew better that I should go with him, so I had to see the consultant on my own and explain what had happened. You have to explain it repeatedly. The consultant was very understanding, but it deeply affected Billy.

It just feels like all medical staff have to work hard to help us overcome it, and it always follows us around. So, no, not really an area where we have moved on much at all.

When you hear what Kelly has to say about dealing with medical issues then it is hardly surprising, but it is an area that hadn't occurred to me. However, anything to do with a potential invasion of her children's bodies will doubtless seem like a threat, and the trauma is somehow reactivated.

As Kelly is talking about something very specific with medical professionals, I am wondering what things are like more generally.

Well, the kids are suspicious of people generally. They do not like people coming into the house. If they do, then they disappear rapidly into their rooms. Friends or family even, they just skedaddle. Vanish. We all stopped having people around. It's easier.

I don't like having doors shut anymore. The bedroom doors are open, so that there is a kind of openness. Behind closed doors no longer happens in our house. When George did have a friend over, I was ever so jumpy in the house. They'd shut the door, I guess because his mate just does that. Most kids would! But within moments of it shutting, I was there, at the door crying, "sweets..." so that I could get in and open it up again. It's really crazy isn't it?

There is also a thing about being late. I get panicky if they are a bit late, as they are with me. I want to know, 'where are you?' So, you end up over estimating how long you might be somewhere, so that you know you'll come back well within what you have said. I know that this is because their dad said to them that I would go missing if they told, so is there a part of them that still believes it? I could disappear at any time. I guess connected to this, is that Billy has to phone and check how everyone is. It's better now, as it used to be about three times a day, but he still does it, without fail. It used to drive me nuts, constantly checking, but I'm used to it now.

The other thing is the youngest hates me raising my voice. You know, you yell a bit as the washing up hasn't been done, and he gets all upset. He hates you losing your temper; reacts badly to it. So, I try not to, but it's impossible. You can't go along in life in this state of calm, and not be riled by things. I do try, but that won't equip him well when he goes out into the world.

I have to be pretty rock solid, and I am generally. I have to be the steady one. It would really frighten them if I were to go into a panic about something, so I've learned to switch off that part of me, a bit. I guess I learned to do that from not reacting to the things they used to tell me. I am good in a crisis. What a consolation!

It seems that the members of the family are still reacting to the sexual abuse in different ways. Ways that, when you think about it, are not surprising, but they seem to be constant reminders. I wonder what impact it has had on Kelly herself, and ask her how she thinks she has been affected.

In different ways. I am a terrible sleeper these days, and I was not always like that. I am so sensitive to everything at night. I am half awake, half asleep. I am not certain that I ever actually sleep. And I'm awake so early. I don't think drugs are the answer, because I need to be one step ahead. I have to be ready for anything. I would love to be able to say, "that was a great night's sleep". I am not sure if that will change.

Then, how I am with other people. It's funny; a friend was teasing me recently, and saying it's been x years since it all happened, and that I've been on my own. Why can't I be on my own? I wouldn't trust anybody now. I am just not interested in being part of a couple. I don't allow anyone in. I keep my distance from people. You've just been hurt so much, and you don't want anyone else to hurt you anymore. So, that's that.

It has affected everything. The way I look at people, try to suss them out. Before I was quite relaxed, easy going. But now, not really. I now start from the position that all men are paedophiles, and they have to prove otherwise. It's horrible, but it's the only way that I can preserve myself.

I comment here that it must be incredibly hard work to carry this attitude around with her. She agrees. It is. Kelly illustrates it by describing how she can be standing in a queue, and notice a child being chided by their dad. She will become alert, and think to herself... 'Ooh, I don't like that'.

I ask her what she will do with that thought.

You can't really say or do anything. You can't say that perhaps that child is being abused, or that man is the abuser. You can't go around accusing people on the street. So, you have to say nothing. Perhaps you might hint at your concern, if it was someone you knew. Like, someone told me that their daughter kept on getting urine infections, and that's what all the kids had when they were small. I said,

"Ooh. I don't like the sound of that. You should keep going back to the doctor with that until they get to the bottom of it. It's not right."

I'd have to do that, but to a stranger. You can't just accuse people. Although my face often betrays me! I have 'a look' apparently, and I don't really want to change that.

KELLY'S STORY

But then how is it to accuse your own children? Kelly is a grandmother, Susie having had a baby a few years ago. Kelly is hyper vigilant around the baby, and is always listening to what the baby has to say. She described her senses as being sharpened. She asks questions – how did you get this bruise, what games did you play today. Kelly feels dreadfully about it at one level, and acknowledges she is overprotective, but her fear is for her grandchild. Her anxiety is deep rooted, that people who have been abused can turn abuser. "It is a risk" she comments, and even though this implicates all of her children, she believes she needs to stay alert to it. Another example of the life sentence that Donald has handed down to her and her children. I am still haunted by this.

With thoughts of the family still affected in many ways, and Donald having perhaps having moved on, I asked Kelly when she thought it would all end.

I don't think it will. Perhaps we will gloss over it one day. Perhaps it will become an unspoken thing in our family one day. I don't really know. I am always on the alert, so I don't think so. I really can't see that it can ever completely go. You don't really want to hide it, but then you don't want to broadcast it either, so you're left in this in between. The life sentence is for the kids, and for me. It just seems to be everlasting.

That said, it is important to Kelly that there is balance in her story. In our last interview, Kelly seemed to be a different woman. There was a lightness about her that I had not previously experienced. She was quite mischievous, playful almost. I was curious as to what this shift has been, and she seemed pleased that I had noticed the change in her.

Kelly is doing things in the last six months that she never dreamed of doing. Partly liberated by the purchase of a satellite navigation system, which has given her confidence to travel further a field. She took her son on a day trip to Southend-on-Sea to buy fish and chips recently. Back then, it would have felt impossible to her.

Her children sent her to Dublin for a weekend with a girlfriend, despite protestations that she 'can't do that'; she did. And what is more, she loved it. She has been bitten by the bug of 'possibility'. Anything is possible now, and she no longer begins from the premise that something is difficult. It is infectious being around her.

KELLY'S STORY

Kelly is desperate to convey the message to anyone in a similar situation that there is light at the end of the tunnel, and that things do improve. She is determined not to become a victim, or watch her children become victims, otherwise he will have won out overall. She knows that she cannot change the past, but she has fought for the right for hers and her children's futures.

Kelly is a remarkable woman.

ASTA'S
STORY

ASTA'S STORY

Asta is a striking woman. She is tall, elegant, and there is something alluring about her. She was generous in giving me a complete story, not hiding from any details or feelings she experienced at times. Yet, at the same time, I sensed a remoteness in her. She does not seem detached, quite the contrary, she is very engaged in her story. I wonder if she protects herself in some way, holds herself back. She considers her responses thoroughly, suggesting a thinking brain. I am left with the impression that she is a very capable and intelligent woman. She seems strong, in a place she has found, but not always where she has been.

Like Kelly, Asta is someone whom you could not imagine going through such traumas. You might even be working alongside her, for her story is buried so deeply that no one around her knows, would have the faintest idea.

Asta spent a lot of time talking to me about her situation long before Freddy, her son, was sexually abused. Her story is complicated, but she feels very strongly that it needs to be explored to explain what she and Freddy have had to deal with. I think she's right. Her and Freddy's story is one that crosses different countries and cultures. It is because of this that Asta has to contend with some very challenging relationships and emotions. Asta begins steadily.

OUR NIGHTMARE

I come from Norway, that's where my family are from. My parents, sister they are still there. It's where I met my husband, and where we lived when we first got married. Freddy was born there, so he's Norwegian too. My husband wasn't Norwegian, a bit different to my Scandinavian roots; he's of Latin blood coming from southern Spain. We were having some difficulties in our marriage, so we decided that we would have a fresh start and try our luck in Spain. It seemed the right thing to do at the time. So, when Freddy was only small, we moved everything and went to live in Barcelona. It was great for a while, and then the problems came back, or they hadn't really gone away, and it seemed worse. I decided that I couldn't stay with him, and so I took Freddy and we went to Germany. I knew some German, and I just couldn't go back home to Norway. I just couldn't admit that everything had gone so wrong. So, for the second time, we started again, this time just Freddy and me. I got work in a hotel and there was a nursery close by. It was going really well. Freddy was settled, and loved going there. I was busy, and the work was flexible so that I could take care of Freddy too. Then, one day, I was due to go and collect Freddy from the nursery, and the phone went. It was my husband saying,

ASTA'S STORY

"You will never see Freddy again."

I could not believe what I was hearing. He had persuaded the nursery to let him take Freddy, and he was driving him across the border back towards Spain. I could not believe it. He had found us, and was taking him from me. He told me that he would be back in two days to collect Freddy's things. I did not trust him, so I went to the hotel manager and told her what had happened, and told her I had to leave. I knew that he would never harm me when Freddy was there, but now he was gone, I thought he was going to come back for me. I was in fear for my life. Right there and then. She agreed to pay me in cash, so I fled to the airport and took a flight to London where my husband would not find me. London was a place I had no connection to, so it was perfect, and I really could not risk going back home. I had one good friend in London, Brigit, so I called her and she said of course I could go there. So that's what I did. She was amazing. I stayed with her at first, and she really helped me. She also had a son, whom I knew from a small baby, from when we were in Norway. She was my saviour, my lifeline. She knew my anguish and was able to really support me. I don't know what I would have done if it hadn't been for her.

I got a job, and then somewhere of my own to live. All the time fighting to get Freddy back. I had no idea where he was. There was no trace of him in Barcelona, or with any of the people I'd know in Spain. My husband's parents had split up, and his father had no idea where his son or wife had gone. It was horrendous. I had a solicitor working for me, but they were useless. Totally useless. It was an awful time, and all I had was my friend and her son, and work. Eventually I got some contact with my husband, and I had to tell him where I was. He said that Freddy wanted to send letters to me, and I had to tell him for the sake of my son. I just had to have some contact with my husband, so that I could reach my son.

One day I came back from work, and I couldn't get my key in the lock. It wouldn't turn. I remember thinking, 'this is weird.' Then the door was flung open, and my husband pulled me in the room, where he completely beat me up. I thought he was going to kill me. I thought I was going to die in this grotty studio flat in London, but I didn't. I ended up in hospital. He'd told some story about being locked out by me, his wife, and a locksmith just changed the lock like that. Cash speaks. He told me again I'd never see Freddy. It was the worst feeling of my life. One of the good things was that the policewoman who dealt with me, she gave me the name of a good solicitor. This solicitor finally got things done, moving. She was really good and she helped me a lot.

ASTA'S STORY

I really didn't think I was going to see Freddy again, and then out of the blue, there was a trace of him. He was in southern Spain, with my husband's mother and her new boyfriend. He was reported to social services there, and they were trying to trace me! He was apparently neglected and missing school, and when he was at school, he was always hungry and stealing food. He was not being cared for, and they wanted to know where the mother was. I could not believe it, and so I went to collect him. I flew over without telling anybody. I did not dare believe that it was true. It was amazing and heartbreaking to see him. He was dirty, long hair, so skinny and smelly, but he was my boy. He was speaking Spanish, a language I did not know, but he was coming with me. I did not dare believe that I was going to be allowed to take him and bring him back with me. I did not dare tell anyone about it. Just as soon as we were through security and had our luggage at Heathrow – that was it. I phoned the world. I just collapsed on the floor and I was crying tears of relief and joy. It was so amazing. My mum came over to see him. It was a really big thing, and we had a real party to celebrate that Freddy was back with me. It had taken two years to get him back.

ASTA'S STORY

Freddy had experienced more upheaval in the first years of his life than many will experience in a lifetime. As I listened to Asta, I was caught up in the dramatic events that had shaped Freddy's first seven years. This seemed to me to be a story in itself, and yet, I knew there was more tragedy to come. This was only the first chapter in his life.

Freddy was at a young enough age where you would hope that back with his loving and caring mother he would flourish. Asta also had endured a great deal of heartache, and subsequently wonders if she had recovered from the trauma of her marriage when Freddy came back into her life. She told me that she watched Freddy like a hawk, as she was afraid that she might lose him again. She was comforted by her friend Brigit and her son; they had a slice of Norway in London. They would spend much time together, helping Asta and Freddy to build a life in London. Asta describes how she found joy again in herself, and she was in the mood to celebrate.

As you can imagine, I was so happy to have Freddy back, and slowly the gap between us closed. He was settling in, and we were able to get along with life. My friend, Brigit, she was a single mum too, but she was a born-again

Christian and wasn't really into partying, and I wanted to go out and go a bit crazy. So I started to go out, and Freddy would go around to their house and stay with Brigit. They have a two storey flat, and her room was downstairs next to the living room while her son Max's was upstairs. Freddy and Max would sleep together, as a sleepover like you do with kids. I didn't think anything of it, they're just kids. Even though Max was older than Freddy, I'd known him since he was a baby, and I thought I knew him. Max was six or seven years older than Freddy, enough of a difference. Freddy was seven and Max was fourteen. Max would turn out to be the person who sexually abused my son.

The way it all came out was that my sister was staying. She was visiting us from Norway, with her husband and two kids; one is almost the same age as Freddy, Ben, just two years difference, and the other was a small baby. I only have a two bedroom flat, so Freddy and Ben were in with me and my sister and her husband were in the other room with the baby. I had just put Freddy and Ben to bed, and I was in the bathroom, and I heard them say,

"Shall we play the sex game tonight?"

It shook me, and I was like, hold on a minute. So, I went into the bedroom and said to them,

95

"What did you just say?"

I needed to find out what this was all about, so I called my sister in to take Ben so that I could talk to Freddy. I said to my sister,

"I think I heard them saying something about a sex game."

So, my sister was talking to her son, and I was talking to mine. We found out that they had been touching each other, like playing, and they called it the sex game. And that's how it all came out.

I regret so much of my reaction, because I reacted so badly. I am really embarrassed about it. I got angry. Really, really angry. Like I could not believe it was happening. I just felt that all the things we'd been through already. It was like. Fucking hell – is there a limit to – you know there's only so much a person can take, and I just could not believe it. I was like. No. Enough is enough. We've been all around the world. I lost him. I fought for him. It took two years to get him back. And I just thought. No. It broke me, and I could not accept it. It was so terrible. I remember being in the kitchen. I didn't want anyone.

"Don't come near me," I was screaming and on the floor. I was screaming and crying. It was so horrible. It was just. No.

ASTA'S STORY

Because I'd lost it so badly, obviously Freddy got so scared when he saw me like that. I spoke to him, and then I broke down again, and then I spoke to him some more. I told him he had to tell me exactly everything that happened. He was so scared of my reaction so I knew he told me the complete truth – I knew nothing he said was a lie. I knew that a seven year old boy could not come up with, you know you don't see things like that on TV, not from your play station. They're not of his world. You don't come up with things like that unless they happened to you. I really believe that every detail came out that night.

I had to know the truth that night, and so I phoned my friend and said that I needed to come over immediately, and that I needed Max to be there too. I wanted to get it sorted, get through it. So my boyfriend's brother drove me to her house. I made him wait outside for me, telling him I had no idea how long I would be but that he had to wait. He did.

I took Freddy with me, and we went inside and sat down. I sat with Freddy on one sofa, and she sat over there with her son, on the other sofa. I said to her,

"Freddy has told me that when he has been here, this is what Max has done to him..."

I did not spare any words. I said everything. I know how hard it must've been for her to listen to that. I know how I felt when I heard it for the first time. Max, he sat there like this *(Asta pulls her body into an upright position with a poker straight face)*. He did not move. But he denied everything. He said,

"No. No. No way. I haven't done anything like that. Bring me the Bible and I'll put my hand on it, and I will swear I've not done anything."

His mum being a newborn Christian - well my friend, the mum, she believed her son. She said that Freddy was confused because he spent time in Spain, and that probably something had happened there. Because he wasn't looked after at all there, and things like that. I just looked at her and thought. No. Freddy had described every single detail. He's not confused. Not at all. I said to her,

"If you don't accept that this has really happened, how can I speak to you, because this has happened to my son?"

We were going to leave, and it was really difficult, because what she did was turn to her son and said to him,

"Look what you've done. I've lost my best friend, we're back together in another country and now I've lost her because of you."

So, for a minute, I thought she does believe it, but doesn't want to accept it. So I thought I would leave it, because it is really difficult to take in. It is really difficult for me, so it must be for her. I phoned her the following day, and she said,

"No, it did not happen. Freddy must be confused with watching the porn on the internet. Maybe it was what they were watching, and maybe what he's seen, and he's confused that it happened to him."

She accepts that they were watching porn in his room, but not that the abuse happened.

I'm not sure how many times it happened. I don't think it happened that many times, but now, looking back, I think I know the first time it happened. It's so terrible, because you know, it's silly I know, but I still blame myself, that I saw something was wrong and I didn't know what it was. I didn't get any answers at the time. I had gone to pick Freddy up, and when I got there, he and Max were still sitting in their pyjamas. It was quite late in the afternoon, which I thought was a bit odd, but I dismissed it thinking they'd just been taking it easy, watching cartoons and being a bit lazy. Every time before he wasn't happy that I'd come back and was taking him home, but there was something different about him that day. He was sat there like this *(Asta changes position to sit bolt upright with both hands placed on her knees).* He wouldn't look at me, and he wasn't normal. No hug. There was such a difference. He was really, well, there was almost like a sadness in him.

My friend's son, Max, starts going to Freddy,

"Come on, say hi to your mum," like he was trying to cheer him up.

Freddy did not do anything; he did not get off the chair. I didn't understand what was going on. Even when we were on the bus going home, I was asking what was wrong, but he said that nothing was. You know, it was only that one time he was like that. So sad.

It carried on like that - when I wanted to go out, Freddy would go there. I'm not sure how long it went on, but he went there a few times more before it all came out.

I know I did sense that something was wrong, but I would never ever in a million years think that my son had been sexually abused the night before. Never ever. You hear stories and they are usually about fat, old, ugly bald men, perverted men, driving a car and you never in a million years think that the abuser is going to be your friend's son.

There is a noticeable shift in Asta as she recalls the circumstances that surround Freddy's abuse, and in particular, his abuser. There is hesitation in her voice, and at times her voice falters, revealing the depth of feeling that she still harbours around the abuse. It is clearly still very painful. This deep emotion touched me, and I was moved to tears by her description of the sadness she sensed in her son, a sadness she was unable to connect to at the time. Asta seemed saddened too. I sense it is about the wish to have done more when she noticed the change in him that afternoon. She still feels that she is to blame for not doing more to understand her son's change in behaviour. Though when I asked her about it, she is not sure that any more questioning on her part would have elicited the truth. She believes, in reality, it would have pushed him further away, but the lingering regret still gnaws away at her. It is evident to me that his abuser was silencing Freddy, and I ask Asta about that.

You know, I felt really sorry for Freddy, and I felt so guilty that I had not noticed. I hadn't seen it happening at all. He was silenced by Max in a very clever way. They had the 'Secret Club.' It was a sex club, but it was very secret and Freddy was not allowed to tell anyone about it. I don't know if he was threatened by Max not to tell, I've never actually asked him about that, but I think it was just this big exciting secret and he really wasn't supposed to tell me. He probably thought it was some big exciting game, like spies, and he really looked up to Max as he was older. He was probably really proud to be included. And then something like that happens to him. It's so sick.

When Asta told me her story, I was disturbed in a way I had not been before, listening to the stories of children who have been abused. When I reflect on it, I think I was deeply affected by the ages of the boys involved in this complicated web of lives, and the connections of their parents that had weaved around them since their own childhood. So much seemed to be surrendered because of their relationships, with somehow, so much more to lose because of it. I ached for each of them tied together in this sordid mess of family, friendship and the betrayal of innocence. How must it have been, trying to hold the position, as Asta did, of mother, sister, aunt, and friend, when each of the ties that bound her to another was stretched and tested? She was also to be tested in her role as daughter, because she had still to pick up the phone and speak to her parents in Norway. I commented that it must have been terrifying to face that conversation with her parents.

You know, at the same time that I was dealing with the situation with my friend, I also had to deal with my family. The atmosphere, it was just awful in my flat, and so after a couple of days they left. They cut their holiday short here with us, and my sister and her family left.

Then I had to speak to my parents. I told them what happened, and it was so very difficult to talk about it. It's terrible even to say those words, and really tell them what has happened. They were very upset. Their initial reaction really shocked me. They said that they wanted to be supportive, and I think in their own way, they were trying to be. They had no experience of this situation, but the actual support that came out was horrible. They initially said,

"You're not really capable of looking after Freddy. So maybe Freddy would be better off somewhere else. Perhaps we could send him somewhere else."

I mean? How could you say that to me? After two years of me having him back, after he was gone for two years, and you want to send him away, to I don't even know where. Where is it you send boys who've been abused to? Where did they think? That's the worst thing in the world you can do for him. All he needs is normality and love and support. Not to be banished to some distant place to be forgotten about. I could not believe what they said to me. I know it was a new situation. I didn't know what to do, what was going on. I was learning every day. Even to have that conversation was so upsetting to me. I thought to myself, 'I don't want to speak to anyone anymore.' I just felt that no one understands how it feels and so it was easier not to speak to anyone because you end up just dealing with everyone else and feeling ten times worse.

I really thought that I would be dealing with this totally on my own. You like to think that you have unconditional love from your parents, and then you question whether it really is. I felt so alone that night. It was so terrifying knowing that what you say will change things forever.

My parents must have really thought about what they had said to me, because the next day they phoned me. My dad then was sounding very strong and stable, telling me that no one was going to be excluded or sent away. My parents went through their own emotions as well, but were trying to be strong for me. My dad also wrote a letter to me to tell me that they were not going to take sides or leave anyone alone. It really made me feel better that they wanted to try to stay strong and stay together and try to get through it.

The unexpected initial reaction from her parents clearly affected Asta greatly. I wonder whether this experience made her wary about sharing this story in the future. If her own parents had reacted so strongly, what judgements might she face from others? Whilst she had the support of her parents from afar, in reality she felt there was no option but to go it alone in London. She severed her ties with her sister and her best friend to focus on her role as mother, and do everything in her power to help her son recover from being sexually abused.

IT'S SUCH A LONELY PLACE

In a short space of time, Asta experienced dramatic and significant changes to her life. Over the course of a weekend, she lost her best friend, her baby-sitter, her sister, her nephew, her parents and the boy she knew as her son. This is an inordinate network of people whom you would ordinarily call on for support who were no longer there. Asta felt very much alone in the world. She spoke openly about her sense of loss.

It was horrible. Really horrible. Losing Brigit was the first thing. This was the friend when I was really in need, when I was scared that someone was going to kill me, when I was in a different country – she helped me out. I felt so bad that I had to say to her,

"I can't speak to you. If you don't accept that this has happened, then I can't speak to you anymore."

I just can't pretend it hasn't happened. For Freddy's sake too. To say that this has happened and we're still friends? No. I can't do it. She was such a dear friend. I still feel only good things about her as a person. I have never said anything bad about her. We have mutual friends and I never say a bad word, and nor does she. We have seen each other a couple of times at functions. I've been nice to her and she's been nice to me, but that's it. We're civilised. But I have lost a really good friend. That was the first horrible thing that came with this. There were many others after that, but that was sort of the beginning of this lonely road. You realise that no one wants to know about it. No one wants to really accept it. It's too painful. It's ... it's horrible how many people you lose really, and how alone you are in this situation. So. Brigit was the first thing.

In that weekend I lost contact with my sister, as I had known it all my life. My son and her son were also like best friends, they had known each other from babies, and so it was so hard that they were both not there. It changed so much. She was obviously disturbed by what had happened to her son, my nephew, but couldn't see that it was very different. My son was severely abused by a much older boy, a boy who should have known right from wrong. My son and her son were like playing, showing, and it was no way the same as the abuse that Freddy suffered. Freddy was too young to understand or talk about what had happened to him, so it was his way of expressing what he'd been shown, made aware of. Nothing like abuse took place, it was like sharing with his best friend. She just could not see that it was not the same. We argued about it a lot. We then couldn't really have conversations about anything, because we were standing so far apart on this one thing. It got in the way of everything. I don't remember which one of us said it, but we agreed that we could not talk anymore. It was too painful. Too raw. So, she went from our lives too.

Asta's feeling of loss was palpable when she spoke to me. I sensed a heaviness in her as she described the impact on her of Freddy's abuse. Her voice slowed down, she sighed more. Because of the change in her, I wondered whether it was the lowest point for Asta, losing her two best friends. I didn't ask her until a later meeting, as I didn't want to detract from her telling her story, her way. She took a deep breath and explored how it affected their everyday lives and her deepening feeling of isolation.

ASTA'S STORY

It just gets worse. You imagine that the worst it will be when you find out. You know my initial reaction was to go kind of crazy, and that's desperate, and wild and raw. But then when you start to realise how much it affects your lives, that's when I found it the hardest to deal with. Because of the way it came out, my sister didn't want Freddy to be anywhere near her son, and that made it difficult to see her. I was so isolated and alone when they went back to Norway. I realised how I was here, in another country, and my sister and my parents were home, together. Everyone was there, and I was here. Completely separate. I felt as if they would say, "don't come here, as we don't want you and your problems."

That was the hardest for me to deal with. We had always been close, a tightly knitted family. I thought that whatever happened to me in the world my parents and my family would be there for me. I shared a bedroom with my sister when we were growing up and we knew everything about each other. We were like best friends growing up. When I used to go back home, we used to go on holiday together every summer, and at Christmas we would all be together as a whole family. I felt I could not go there. If I went to my parents', then I felt like my sister's family couldn't go there. I felt that I was just not part of that family anymore.

So, we didn't go for Christmases. We just couldn't go. So I stayed here with Freddy for a few Christmases. Summer holidays were different; because they are longer we could avoid having to be there at the same time. I did try to speak to my sister the first summer to see if we could make it work. But there was no way that she was going to let those kids, cousins, see each other. The conversation once again was going nowhere. My parents would have my sister's kids first, and then when they had gone, Freddy and I would go over. It was really awful, the divide, but I really wanted to see my parents. In some ways it keeps on reinforcing the pain, but I really wanted to go home. I needed to go home.

I was struck by the unbearable tension of this situation. It seemed to be a completely insoluble problem. The pull of wanting to see her parents, having Freddy spend time with his grandparents, being free of the isolation she experienced in London against the opposite pull of feeling alienated from her sister and the sense of family that she had known before. It was as if it still lived around them – the abuse that had taken place and had ended was still infiltrating their lives. I was beginning to understand Asta more, and why the lowest point was not when she broke down, faced with the truth for the first time. Asta continued to explore the effect it had on them.

So. I had lost my two best friends. You go to work and there you might be able to have a moan or complain about something like, "oh my boyfriend irritated me last night..." but this was not one of those problems that I could complain to people about. So it was really lonely for me. A lonely, empty horrible place. I really felt like this was the hardest, to be on my own.

You know, I could not tell anyone about it. I was still going through the court, with my ex-husband for the divorce and to get sole custody of our son. You know despite the fact that Spanish social services had been involved with Freddy having to be repatriated to me, I still had to do this in court. And my ex-husband was being so nasty, saying all kinds of things, like I was a prostitute, a drug user, and all kinds of things to undermine me. So I could not let anything jeopardise that. I thought, 'Oh My God. If this comes out. No way. It can't.'

I didn't dare tell the police, or social services, or even Freddy's school. He was out of the risk of danger from the abuser, and it was my job to protect him. I was the only one who could.

There is one feeling that I had, which was when I was at rock bottom. I am so ashamed of this, and I have never spoken it out loud to anyone. It is horrible for me to even say it now, but I was upset with Freddy for a while. Upset with him that he's done this. And of course I know that it's not his fault in any way, but I could not help these feelings. All of this that was around us; that I'd lost my sister, my family, everything. Everything was suddenly so difficult. I knew I had to get away from those feelings. I felt so guilty for having those feelings of being upset with Freddy. I'm such a horrible mum, but in all honesty, I did feel like that. I was disappointed in my son. God. Such a horrible thing to say, as he was only a child. I felt I had to justify my son's being, and his right to be in this family - to my parents as well. I was all over the place with my feelings. It was awful, a really awful place. I am very ashamed of this now, to have these feelings, but it is the truth.

I knew I just had to pull myself together, and so I contacted Mosac, really only a short time after the abuse had come tumbling into our lives. I knew I was in such a state and I knew I had to deal with it. I thought, 'I am the only one who can look after Freddy. He has no one else. I am the only person and I have to pull myself together. So, I have to learn about this. I have to deal with this. I have to know how to speak to my child who has been abused. How to deal with him.'

I went for a kind of assessment, and they told me that this was a place where I didn't need to hide. I didn't have to carry this dark secret on my own. Mosac is not connected to the police or the government, and so I felt safe that they would not tell anyone about us. This was the place I could talk about what had happened and what was going on.

I didn't know anything about sexual abuse, so at the same time as I was working on me, I had to educate myself. I spent a lot of time on the internet. I got some books, and some booklets from Mosac. One of the most useful was about how to communicate about sex, and if your child has the urge to touch themselves. It was really useful. Straightforward for dealing with something that's so not straightforward.

The therapy was difficult. I had to get some help because I was devastated about everything and I was all over the place. I was lost and I can remember feeling scared that I couldn't look after my child. I had messed up so badly already and then it was happening again. I was really having doubts about myself as a mother. I thought that I just couldn't do it anymore. Just when you think that the worst has happened in your life, even worse happens – worse because it's so bad that you don't even have nightmares about it. It's beyond what you worry about as a parent. Beyond nightmares. Something you don't even imagine and then something that bad happens. On top of everything else. My therapy wasn't just about Freddy's abuse, but everything as well. Actually, mostly it was about me. I had to go through everything – I wanted to go through everything – to sort it all out. To kind of repackage myself. Like I've sat with you and told you about everything, so that you can understand. You have to understand the whole story so that it all makes sense. You have to be able to make some kind of sense of it so that you can be strong again. I didn't get any practical advice from the therapist. That's not how therapy works. It was a long process to get myself together really, it took about a year. It's funny. One day I just stopped talking. I just looked at the therapist and said,

"I've said everything. What do we do now?"

So that was the end of my therapy. It was a long process. A very long process. It was very hard.

ASTA'S STORY

Asta was laughing at times as she was telling me about the process of therapy. She does that at times when she is telling her story. I had noticed this before, but chose this point to share my observation, that she was laughing often when the story seemed to reach a new level of tragedy or difficulty. She looked at me, and replied,

"I've cried so much, and I'm feeling a bit tearful now. And I'm trying to hold it together so that I can tell you what has happened. And when you start crying, it's non-stop. It's laugh or cry. If I cry, I won't be able to talk anymore, so I'll try to stay strong."

I was deeply moved by Asta. She was being so generous with me, not only sharing her story but her reflections on herself in the moment with me. I found myself filled with enormous respect and tenderness for this resilient woman, and complete admiration for her as a mother.

From here, Asta turned her focus towards Freddy, both with how he had been in the aftermath of the abuse he had suffered, how she was with him.

I said before that I didn't know if I had to do anything differently with him. I didn't know how to react with him.

How do you deal with him? He was really young at the time, and he did not understand what was going on. At seven you're a child and should not be in the adult world of sex. I was really worried about him, and whether he would act on what he had experienced and continue with it. There were so many things I was now worried about that I hadn't been before. I thought to myself that I could not even go to anyone's house. I can't let him stay over at anyone's place, or I can't even let children come here. It was such a lonely place, suddenly you feel like you're locked up from the whole system. You don't imagine some of the things that you are going to be feeling and worrying about. I was involved in another project with Mosac, and I was listening to another woman's story, about her grown up son. It's shocking actually, but she did not trust her grown up son around children. And I can remember thinking, 'OH MY GOD! I don't want to live like that!'

I don't want to go on when he's growing up thinking that I cannot leave my son with another child. I don't know. There must be a way out of this. Not every child who is abused becomes an abuser, I know that, but I knew I had to find a way that I could help Freddy deal with what he had been through, to help him learn the right way from the wrong way.

ASTA'S STORY

The first year after it happened, he was really struggling. At his school it felt like I was in the head teacher's office every week. Freddy's done this. Freddy's been in a fight. He hit this person. He did this. He did that. He was always getting into trouble. I was having therapy at Mosac, but I really wanted some help for him, and when I asked them (Mosac) to help him, they couldn't. They didn't have anything for children then. I really knew it was up to me to get myself together so that I look after my son. Only I couldn't help him when he was at school, getting frustrated by other children. When Mosac told me that they had won some funding to start play therapy, I was so relieved. Freddy was able to have a place there. He's been there for two years now, and he absolutely loves it. He really does. I think it took him quite a long time to get into it. I was worried about that; I knew that he would take a while to trust the space, trust the play therapist. But now. No problems. It's his own space. He loves it. It's where, well, it's a safe space for him to express all his anger and all that. I don't really know what happens there, and I don't need to know. I just need to know that he's safe. The play therapist really reassured me, advised me how to be with him through this process. She said to me not to ask him any questions about the therapy, so we don't really talk about it. Sometimes he tells me, but it's up to him. I do not ask him. Not like I would normally, when I'll tell him what happened to me in my day at work, and I'll ask him,

"So, what happened today, how was the maths test?"

You know what I mean. If he wants to tell me about the therapy, he will. If not, he doesn't. Oh the space is so important to him. It's so sweet. It's going to end soon, but I think he's ready to move on.

I understood, and completely supported the notion that Freddy's therapy was his own process, and believe Asta has done a wonderful thing in holding that boundary for him. At the same time, I was curious about how the play therapy had affected Freddy. The changes that Asta had observed in Freddy for herself, and those that he communicated to her. I asked her this question.

Absolutely I have noticed changes in him. There's definitely a difference with Freddy. It has really helped him. He doesn't get into fights, and he's very good with violence. He's very tall and stocky for his age. He's not fat, but he's a big build and big for his age. He told me the other day,

"Sometimes other boys want to fight me, but I just don't want to fight with them. You know, there's too much fighting and violence and wars, Mum. I don't want to fight."

He has such a peaceful little soul in a giant big body. For him to say that, well I think it's really good. You know, we are so close now we can talk about anything. After the initial shock that I went through, and through the process of getting myself back together, we have talked about this a lot. About the abuse, with real words, real things. All the things that have happened. We've cried about it. Felt abandoned because of it. We've been sad together. We've missed people together. All of those things. We've both been really honest about everything. And I feel really good about Freddy. Today we are in the place where we are, and he is really honest with me. He knows that if he has any worries he can come and talk to me. He does feel safe with me, even after that whole episode of my breaking down, and I really appreciate that. He has really changed. It's horrible what has happened to him, and I think obviously something will stay in him, in me too, but we have recovered a lot. I never thought we might get to this place. Of course it's devastating, and I wish it had never happened, but it did happen, and we have had to recover from it.

Sometimes I feel like, when I found out, it was like something died. You'll never have it back and it's gone. You have a mourning process. Then you have a birthday, an anniversary of the day you found out, and you have a Christmas. You're kind of grieving what was, for him too, for what he was, and all of that innocence is gone. Shock-horror drops on you like a bolt of lightening. It drops from the sky and it knocks you down. Your child is gone. You were seven. Bang! Now you're an adult. Deal with it.

Asta and Freddy have clearly worked hard to recover from their experience of childhood sexual abuse. Much of the work they have done with the support of the professionals at Mosac, but they have worked together too. They were also helped by the reconciliation of their family, which Asta relates in her final chapter.

THE ROAD TO RECOVERY

Asta's road to recovery was one that took several years. She measures recovery in terms of the contact with her family, and the pattern of family life returning to how they had been. Even though they maybe geographically remote, which increased her sense of isolation, it was the feeling that she and Freddy no longer belonged that hurt the most. These days, her story is different.

It all happened quite gradually really, and it's hard to pinpoint an exact time when you realise you're well and truly on this road. I think the point where change first began to take place was when I had begun my therapy, when I was getting stronger. After Freddy had help, definitely that made a big difference, and I had some feedback from his time in play therapy. I was still getting really down about my family, these conversations that were going nowhere with my sister. Then one day something almost snapped in my head. It was another conversation when we were arguing, and I said to her,

"I love my son and we are a family together. If you don't want to see him, then you cannot see me either."

Eventually I felt strong enough in myself that we could be strong together. I felt like I was really fighting for Freddy and me. It was a real change in me. I don't know, but I think it really helped me to overcome those feelings that I was having. Suddenly I was screaming inside about how anyone could speak to me like that. I was the one who changed. It was the real start to our recovery.

Of course we, me and my sister, did talk to each other but it was incidentally and very superficial. Like a "hi, how are you?" nothing deep or related to the abuse. She didn't want to know anything about Freddy at all. I continued to speak to my parents all the time, just as I had done before, and each time I learned something, I told them about it. I have to say that they no longer think that you should send a child away who has been sexually abused. Such silly things come to your mind, but they really don't think that now. I told you that the support they gave me initially was not good support. It wasn't, but over the years they have been really good. It made the difference when we did go over there, to Norway. When we go there, they really show us love. To me and Freddy, both of us. It is fantastic.

ASTA'S STORY

It was last summer, 2008, when things really changed. I had taken Freddy to Norway to spend some time with my parents, and I did not even bother to get those kids together. I did not try, as I was tired of being pushed away. We were going go-karting to celebrate Freddy's birthday, and his cousin loves go-karting, well anything about cars really. My mum was on the phone to my sister telling her, and she said,

"Oh, that sounds really good. I think Ben would like to do that too. Do you think you could pick him up?"

I thought, 'Oh. OK.' That was nice. One big step for her, but a step closer. So, we went to pick Ben up and it was so amazing. I remember it so clearly. We were waiting at the car for him to come down, and he comes down. We are waiting at the car, and I haven't seen this boy for four years and he comes down. He was so happy.

A couple of years before, my sister had told me,

"You know, Ben does not want to see you..."

"No. No way. We have always been close, and this is your stuff. This is not true and I don't believe you. We are not having this conversation..." That was that.

You could see those two boys when they saw each other how it wasn't true. Ben not wanting to see us? I just knew it wasn't true. Their faces lit up when they saw each other and they ran to each other and gave each other a big hug. It was so great. The boys sat in the back of the car. Freddy speaks English and some Norwegian, Ben speaks Norwegian and a bit of English, but they had their own language going on about football, the play station. It was like all that time had vanished. All that time they never saw each other just wasn't there. It was such a happy moment. I was quite tearful sitting in the front seat of the car. It was very emotional. Such a great day. We took Ben back home, and the next day he came out with us again, this time with his younger brother. So slowly it started from there. Eventually they came over to my parents' house and they were allowed to play together. It was just ... well ... back to normal.

Last Christmas we went back for the first time, and my sister was there with her children and it was just so nice. We stayed up until six in the morning playing board games with the boys. It was lovely.

I really feel we have overcome so much, you know. All the horrible time we went through. Obviously it is something that will always stay in Freddy, it's part of him. He's probably going to have problems in the future because of it, but at least we have come through something already. We learned about it. I think we've been through the worst now. It's not that scary anymore.

ASTA'S STORY

I was intrigued by the notion that the experience was no longer scary to Asta. It had not really occurred to me that the experience had been scary. Horrible and lonely had been the feelings that had struck me most in listening to Asta, and I wanted to understand more about this.

It has been scary at times. Because you're so in the dark about how best to handle it, you're afraid that you might make it worse. Also, you have no idea what is coming around the corner. I had believed that I had experienced the worst that life could throw at me in the time I was fighting and waiting to get Freddy back, but it wasn't the case. I was afraid that more terrible things might happen. I was scared of doing the things we used to do. I didn't want to make things worse for Freddy. It is the great number of unknowns that become frightening, I think made worse because I felt so alone. I didn't know what was 'normal' for someone in my situation, Freddy's situation. It's like we had to learn to live again. It also became less scary because I could see positive changes in Freddy as a result of his play therapy as well as knowing I was stronger

125

as a result of mine. As I became stronger, I was more able to deal with things as well as becoming more able to support him directly.

It took a lot of strength in both of us to be able to talk about it openly. You know, not beating about the bush about anything. Being honest that it happened. Me telling him that I was so sorry it happened to him, that it is not his fault, that he is very brave. I cannot tell you enough how close we are, and how open he is with me. I feel very close to him, which helps me so much. I do feel better knowing that he's being honest with his feelings. He's a very emotional boy, but very sensible too. I always tell him that there will be times when he feels down or a bit tearful but that he may not know why. It is traumatic and it will come out in different ways for him. I tell him not to be afraid of it, but to come home and we'll try to talk about it, sort it out or make sense of it. I tell him to be aware of it, and not to just tell everyone about it. I have told him it's his own private story and that people won't always understand or be very kind. I think he knows that from his own experience though. He saw how it affected us so he knows the reality of how people reacted around us. He was actually never inclined to tell anyone about it.

It's funny. It's OK for me to talk about it now, to you. I'm quite surprised really because I don't really talk

about it to other people. To come here and realise that I
can talk about it and be OK is really good. It shows me
how I have recovered so much from it.

I was very touched by Asta's realisation of her own
progress. Story telling is a very powerful tool and can be a
process in its own right to lay everything out and make
sense of things. Asta, in recalling her own story, was able
to not only to present the narrative of what had happened,
but also use it to assess her own journey and the growth
that she has achieved. Believing in Asta's strength, I
wanted to explore with her the nature of her painful
journey and the time it had taken. I asked her if she
thought that she had to wait for time to pass or whether
she could have made things, progress, come any quicker.

No. I think you have to give yourself time first of all. It's
such a shocking thing to happen to you, and you won't just
recover overnight. You don't even get used to it overnight.
It does take time for it to sink in even, and then you begin
the slow process of learning to live with it and then to

recover from it. Even when you begin to read about it, to try to understand it, it's not enough. It's such a big thing to take in that you have to allow yourself time to process it in your own head. Then you will hopefully see some development, that things don't get to you so much, or that you notice some behaviour change. You realise that you're more confident or your child is. You notice that they are smiling and are happier as you move away from it. You begin to believe that there is light at the end of the tunnel because what your child feels, you feel. If they are in the dark place, then you are, but when they start to come out you do. You both have to believe that you will recover. That's very important, and has to happen at its own speed. And then the people around you, my family in my case. Just as it takes you time to deal with it, so it does for them. There is no point in trying to make someone see what you see, like my sister. She had to get there at her own pace, and the hard bit is waiting for them. Not jumping down their throat for not getting there sooner. It is very hard, but you have to learn this super patience.

I reflect to Asta that she seems incredibly grounded and realistic, which seem to me are vital qualities in aiding recovery. It also occurs to me that there is still an unknown around the corner with the approach of puberty for Freddy.

Yes, this is starting for him already. This is the reason that he has to end play therapy. He's moving away from being a young child, and the play therapist doesn't feel it's right for him anymore. I would love for him to stay in that space, and he really wants to continue, but you have to listen to the professionals. You know it's nice to be a child and not grow up too much. The world is still very scary at times, and with all the hormonal changes in him, it's unsettling. You know, sometimes he can be so very childish, like such a small baby. And he's big and muscly - much heavier than I am - and sometimes he wants to sit on my lap like a baby and have me rock him. Then there are days when he really behaves like the man of the house, he's trying to fix things or carry in the heavy bags. He has those two extremes. It must be very hard for him as they are very strong emotions and there is no nice middle ground. It's one or the other.

I feel cautious about the future at times. All these stories you hear about paedophiles and serial killers - a lot of them seem to have been abused. So when your child is abused you think, well, is that the future for him as well? What worries me, you know, is when I'm not there, not able to guide him to go in the right direction. Is he going to stay on the right path? We don't know that really about our children. You do your best to advise them and show them as much as you can to do the right thing. But you know that's one of the hardest things as parents what we have to do, to let go. Let them be their own individuals. Deep down I know that Freddy will be OK, as we still talk about it to this day when he needs to. We are very open with each other, and I know that he does know the difference between what is right and what is wrong. Like I said, he's a very sensitive and sensible boy.

However, it's a fear that still lingers at times. Yes it is a fear, but it's something in time you learn to live with it as well. I think that's what it is now for me. It's a horrible thing to have happened to Freddy, especially on top of what he's been through already. It feels so unfair. I try not to think about the impact too much, because it's just too painful. I can't take the time back, so I have to accept it. I have to force myself to accept it. I can't change it. It's happened. You can get crazy if you think, 'what if'. You can't get crazy. Goodness knows I did that, but it gets you nowhere, so you have to learn to stop doing that. You have to accept the reality of it.

The degree of honesty about the situation is something that comes out strongly when I talk to Asta about her experiences, and how she has overcome it. I am certain that this can only help her son deal with his future. She knows that he is coping better with his own feelings, and because he is growing up, he is more able to talk about things.

Obviously Freddy is no longer a small child, and therefore he can talk about things more, whereas when he was younger, he just was not able to talk and make sense of things. He's much more able as a 12 year old than a 7 year old. He just doesn't punch people when something frustrates him. He's learned to walk away and resolve it another way. I am hoping that us being open, finding a space to deal with it, talk about it, rather than just act on an impulse. He's more confident in himself, as I said. I know I'm OK, but seeing him being OK. That's important.

I wonder if it's the same for him too, maybe he does feel the same. Maybe it's mutual.

I don't know about the future. I don't think it's the last time he'll be in therapy because of this, but for now, I think we have come through something. I hope it gives him confidence for the future, that therapy did help him once, so that if he did need some help in the future, he'd seek it out. Some people think you need to be a bit of a lunatic to have therapy, but it's not the case. It just helps you sort things out in a space that's safe. There's a stigma for that, for therapy, which doesn't help. But I think he'll know it really helped him.

One of the things that I was really missing was being 'normal', the normality of life. That was one of the things I really learned going through therapy. I mean what is normal? I learned that there isn't normal. I kept saying to the therapist that I wanted "a normal life... a normal boring life." There is a part of me that still wants that. People look at me when I complain about it, and say,

"But your life, it's so exciting, going here and there..."

I think to myself, 'if only you knew the price it comes with.' All the time we were going through this, I had to keep working. It was my survival. My 'normality.' I work in the beauty industry, so it's all about pretty things, nice things. I had to work, as it was just Freddy and me so there was no choice, but I'm glad I had to. It takes your mind off things, and how good was it to escape the trap of your mind? I was able to be free of it for eight hours a day. Oh my God. That was so important to me. I really miss the normality of life. But you can't have your time back, so you have to try to get used to life as it is. I think that Freddy and me have got our lives back; we have a 'new normality' now, which really helps. We have routines in our life again. They make you feel safe.

Normality is a strange thing to yearn for, it seems to me, but I understand Asta's desire to return to the familiar rather than face the unknown. I comment to her that for a while it must be that their world changes - where the abuse becomes the centre of everything in that she's trying to hold it, contain it, keep it secret, keep going because of it. And then slowly, it moves out of focus; so that you can find your routines again, go swimming or whatever it is. Asta takes up this image.

Yes, because every experience you have you look at in a different light because this abuse, it become the centre of everything you have to navigate around. Like going to the swimming pool. It becomes a question first of all. Is this something we can do? It becomes a massive step. Can I take my son here? Can we do it? Will someone notice us differently? Then you build up the courage to do it, and then you do it. And when it's all fine, it gives you a kind of confidence, and that particular anxiety moves to the side. In the beginning there was always something else to take its place, but it becomes less. After going through the steps of doing things again, for the second or third time, you realise that there are things that you can do, and you kind of find your normality again. Then you find there have been days when you realise you haven't thought about it at all. You go to a place together, and you come back, and you realise you didn't think about it at all. You weren't cautious or hyper vigilant. You feel happy and you can laugh. You know there is a time when it doesn't shadow you every day. That's when it really starts to become clear that we are well on this road to recovery. It's very gradual though, but you do get there.

As you can probably imagine, leaving my son with someone else was a really big one to overcome. I was like -

is this it for the rest of my life until he moves out? But we are there already on this one.

I wanted to know how Asta felt she had changed because of the experience that she and her son had gone through. I know that she had noticed changes in her son's behaviour, initially with his behaviour deteriorating but then in his recovery. But how does it affect someone who is an adult, with a fully formed personality? There is lots of evidence here that Asta has become stronger, but how else has she changed?

This experience has certainly shaped me, as all experiences do of course. In a way I'm much more relaxed about things. That sounds quite strange, doesn't it? But if something happens, I don't get so stressed about it because I know it's not the end of the world. I have told you I am stronger in myself, but I don't always feel like that, and at the time it all came out, I felt that I had no strength at all. But in having to pick myself up and put myself back together again; well you learn something about yourself in that process. I learned to respect and love myself. Also not to be so hard on myself - that was quite a process too. After the end of my marriage, my self-esteem was very low. After years of all that abuse from my ex-husband. You know I don't think I was in a good place when it all came out with Freddy, as I was still recovering from the damage of my marriage. Perhaps it made it a longer process for our recovery? I don't know.

I know myself much more these days. I am much calmer. I think people might say that about me. I love getting older and I love this place where I am right now. I have lines on my face, but I am comfortable where I am right now. It's nice getting older, wiser and knowing more about the world. You know I don't judge people, or I try not to. You don't know what happens to people, why they are why they are. I come from a very safe, secure background. A good family but it doesn't mean that that's it for life. You really don't know what's going to come at you. It's nice to realise that. It helps. At the same time, I am quite sensitive these days to the suffering that is in the world. It hurts me. I feel emotional pain more that I would have done before all this. I guess I am more open to it. I have strong empathy with people in trouble.

ASTA'S STORY

There is one huge change in me – what ifs? I don't do those anymore, and oh yes, I did it a lot. I beat myself up badly about absolutely everything. My failed marriage. It's all my fault. I'm such a bad mother. This needn't have happened to Freddy, to us. Oh there are many things I could punish myself for. I try not to do that anymore. It's my life and I have lived it this way. It's not easy, and I still go back to those dark moments sometimes. But I also learned how to come out of those dark places. A lot of positive affirmations to yourself. Distracting techniques. Yoga. Work. Running. Wine. Sleeping tablets if I'm in a really bad place. I used to have terrible dreams, but I learned to control my dreams. I was always running away from something, somebody, and I would wake up terrified. But I learned to control them. To face your fears in your dreams. When you're awake you have to tell yourself how you are going to react and cope in your dream. You have to know what it is you are going to do, so that in the dream you do it. You are strong enough. You are going to stop running and turn around and face them. It is so scary in a dream to do this. But you do it, and when you turn around there is no one there anymore. I have never had this dream again, but it took me a long time to be able to turn around and face it.

ASTA'S STORY

At the same time, there are things I look back on and wish I had done differently. A few things. My initial reaction. I wish I could take that back. I also wish I didn't have those feelings that I had towards my son. I was upset with him, but how could I be? I have also learned you can't just live in the past, and wish that things had been differently. You can't change things. You can't take things back and you can make yourself crazy in the process of trying to change the past. That is the hardest, one of the hardest things. To be able to stand there and accept,

"There are things I cannot change."

Asta's story is moving, and I remain deeply impressed by her - her strength, courage and humility. I cannot help but think that Freddy is very blessed to have Asta for his mother. Asta's fight for herself and her son has been largely one that she has faced alone. She wants to convey a message that recovery begins with work on yourself, as an individual. I make this point explicitly for Asta, but I believe her testimony illustrates it better than I can state for her.

In closing Asta's story, I want to share something of her name. In searching for the name that I would use to

138

ASTA'S STORY

protect her identity, I came across 'Asta'. It means 'star' and 'love'; I think it suits her perfectly.

LAUREN'S
STORY

LAUREN'S STORY

Lauren is an attractive woman. She is sharp, intelligent and fiercely proud of her daughters. She used to be trusting of people, but no longer is. The warmth and caring nature have been eroded from her by the hurt that has been caused. Lauren's life, and the lives of her daughters, has been scarred by the man they would call 'Dad'.

Lauren was taken in by him, and she wants you, the reader, to have a real picture of a sexual predator. This is the special chapter that I referred to in my introduction.

In this chapter, I refer to child sex offenders as "he" for ease of reading. It also sits with the chapter's context - it being a man who sexually abused Lauren's children.

LAUREN: A WOMAN GROOMED

It is almost unimaginable that someone would want to prey on children for friendship, intimacy and sex, and the question that emerges when you go there is, what are they like? The media stereotype of the child sex offender probably reflects what most of us would perceive to be the type of person who sexually abuses children. Our newspapers hail them as 'monsters', presenting us with grainy images of the men looking their worst. Think of Josef Fritzl or Roy Whiting. These images feed the stereotypes that we carry.

At Mosac, during our training in child sexual abuse, we were led to explore these stereotypes, the descriptions of child sex offenders: 'Sad', 'isolated', 'hostile', 'creepy-looking', and 'perverted' were the words we chose. We were unanimous in describing the monsters that the media have given us. However this image is dangerously far from the truth. In 2002, BBC2 screened a documentary called "The Hunt for Britain's Paedophiles", showing the work of the Paedophile Unit of The Metropolitan Police. It makes harrowing viewing. In the book of the same name, on the back cover jacket is written:

LAUREN'S STORY

"Monsters don't get close to children, nice men do..."

This is the true face of a paedophile, a child sex offender.

All of the contributors in this book have had their stereotypes of child sex offenders brutally shattered, to their own cost. All have commented to me that they are not as you would believe from coverage in the media. The real threat to children is not from stranger danger, but from those that have eased themselves into the heart of the families. The child sex offender is not just the balding, lonely old man in a raincoat standing at the edge of the park. He is someone that you and your children have come to trust, and he is welcomed in your home.

I can remember being introduced to the term 'grooming' on a training course, thinking it was a strange choice of phrase. My initial thoughts were about the process shared by chimpanzees, complete in my mind with a soft David Attenborough voice over. For me, grooming was about a gentle process, and it seemed a million miles away from the world of paedophilia and the sexual abuse of children. Like the people I have interviewed, I once believed that children were snatched off the streets to be abused.

LAUREN'S STORY

The statistics we have do not bear this out. They are complicated, but the NSPCC[9] estimated that 16% of children experience sexual abuse in childhood. Of that 16%, only 5% suffer at the hands of people not known by the child. The inference being that most sexual abuse is committed by someone known to the child. That child is 'groomed' for sex by a child sex offender, and as part of that process of grooming the child, the parent is also often deceived and manipulated into handing over access to their children. The child sex offender will befriend the child in a non-sexual and a sexual way, and the nicer he is then the less risk there is that the child will tell when his attentions switch to sexual activity. The child sex offender will then keep the child in this abusive relationship by whatever means he needs to - for Kelly's son George, it was threats that George would be killed. For Lauren's daughter Sophie, it was drugs and alcohol and the promise of a life together. For Asta's son Freddy, it was the privilege of being in a secret club. For these children the power exerted over them by the abuser was persuasive and persistent. But in each case, the veil of deceit was also extended to their parent who was also taken in by the abuser. None of

---

[9] In Cawson, P., Wattam, C., Brooker, S. and Kelly, G. (2000) Child maltreatment in the United Kingdom: a study of the prevalence of child abuse and neglect. London: NSPCC.

them saw the dark side of the love and friendship that was offered. It is very true of the child sex offender that they really do only reveal what they want you to see.

Lauren is very forthcoming with the details of her story as she is keen to show how she was taken in by the man that would become the abuser of her children. She wants to warn other single mothers what a sexual predator of children looks and behaves like. I would defy anyone to be able to spot a child sex offender on the streets, but the pattern of behaviour is alarmingly similar. It is these signs that Lauren wants to alert you, the reader to.

Lauren expresses her concerns very clearly; the reasons why we want to dismiss this as a possibility. She says,

"No one wants to believe a human being is capable or desirous of having sex with a child, but it happens. It happened to both of my children. Because of the sex offenders register, those people who want to target children are having to operate in different ways. It is harder for them to work, or volunteer, where there are children - like schools, youth clubs, and scout and brownie groups - therefore they have to work their way into the family to access a child. It is shocking, and people do not want to believe it is taking place, but it is. It really is. Child sex offenders are working on single mums - they are being targeted, so that they can access their children, and even father their own to get parental responsibility so that they really have control and authority over their child."

Lauren's warning is to other single mothers, to be careful of whom you allow into your house. One of the things that unites child sex offenders is that they are nice, *very* nice - they will be great around your children and make themselves indispensable to you. They are also adept at manipulation. They will complicate situations and stir up feelings so that the victim (both the child and parent) is rendered confused, and often helpless, making it hard for that victim to be able to tell what is happening to them. They will hurt you and your children on many levels. This perhaps sounds cryptic, but Lauren's story illustrates it very well.

Lauren tells me how she was taken in by Rob.

I was already a mum to Sophie when I met Rob - she would have been four or five. Her dad had long vanished from the scene, so it was just Sophie and I. He didn't pay any maintenance; he wasn't nasty, he just wasn't around. I was working, I had my own house. I was at university. I was so proud of myself for achieving this, as I was severely dyslexic, so it was huge for me. Life was good, and I felt great. Sophie had just started school and I was having to do several jobs to pay the bills and fit in my studies. Because of all of this, I wasn't actually looking for a relationship at all. I think everyone goes through a phase in his or her life of being quite needy and desperate to be in coupledom, but I wasn't there at all. I was feeling really strong and where I wanted to be.

The people across the road moved out, and someone I'd known at school moved in, not exactly a friend but more like an old acquaintance. She and her husband moved in, and we became more friendly. Rob hung around with them. Then he started hanging around me a bit. It all began with silly things, like if I was cutting a hedge then he'd be there at my side offering to help out. I didn't dislike him as he was nice enough, but there was just something about him I didn't really warm to. My neighbours were pushing me towards him, but I kept saying that there was something that didn't gel with me. I couldn't explain it though, and because I couldn't explain it, the pressure was kept on. This went on for a very long time, probably around a year and a half - he would just come and be really useful and hang out for a bit and be generally very helpful and pleasant. He even introduced me to his family who would drop him off at his friends' every now and again. They seemed really lovely. His father was a vicar and as I am a Christian, his family being Christian appealed to me. I liked the way their family seemed so close and that influenced how I saw Rob. His kind and devoted family was definitely a selling point for him. Eventually he asked me out, he asked a few times, and I'd say,

"You know Rob, I'm not really in for a relationship, I'm busy, I have all these things going on...." I didn't want to date.

There was this constant pressure from friends and my family for me to get together with him. "How can you possibly not want to be with Rob", or "Oh, he's so lovely", and "He'd be so good for you!" And then it turned to,

"Lauren, you know Rob really likes you. You're on your own and you are struggling at times, and you don't have to. You may think you're doing fine, but I know you, and I'm not so sure. You need someone in your life. You need a man in your life".

These comments subtly dented my confidence and my faith in how I was doing. They made me question my own views on whether I was coping. Knowing what I know now, I would hazard a guess that he'd been telling stories to people about how I wasn't coping, and because they cared about me, they would say something to me. Unfortunately it works - if you question someone enough they will start to doubt themselves.

I was worked on so gently. God, he was so nice, not directly pushy at all. I didn't fancy him, and there was this niggle that there was something about him I didn't like, but then he was being so helpful, so nice. What's not to like about someone who is gentle and generous - helping with the shopping from the car, or helping to fix a car? There was nothing to dislike, so that feeling I had seemed ridiculous.

He was persistent, and one day it worked when he said,

"Look, just come for an evening out, a couple of drinks, you need to get out because you're doing so many things."

I agreed to go on a couple of dates with him, which were fine, but then it was just assumed that we were partners. Instead of going to see his friends, my neighbours, he was coming to see me. At the time, I felt I was going a bit mad, and I wanted to say to him,

"Look, you just can't come around when you want to, I want you to call me first..." But of course, I didn't say anything more to him. I felt silly and mean; it was a good thing that he liked me so much wasn't it?

LAUREN'S STORY

When it got too much, I'd try and make light of it and say,

"Look Rob, I'm not up for marriage just yet..."

He'd act all hurt and say that he didn't want to push me, but that he really liked me, and I felt so terrible, so guilty. Really guilty. Also, I'd have my neighbour coming over and saying to me,

"What have you done to Rob?"

I felt that my options were to end the relationship, based on nothing much bad really, or to keep the relationship. He wasn't leaving any middle ground for me to work with. So I'd looked at him, and got to thinking that he wasn't so bad. The dialogue inside my head went something like,

'Where is this doubt coming from? I am the nutter! I am mad. I obviously have no taste in men, because if I had, then I wouldn't have married the first one. It must be me. It is me. He's a good guy.'

I ended up slowly getting drawn into a relationship with this man. In the end he was so nice, so sweet, and so helpful - you know when you get used to someone being around? Even though I struggled with him in the first place, I learned to negotiate and navigate around him, so it worked a bit more. And that's the way it happened. It was bizarre. Even from the start I questioned my own sanity because everyone else was so into him. It was very hard for me not to say to myself, 'I am the one with the problem.'

There we were, we were a couple. "Lauren and Rob". His conversation soon turned to children, and he was constantly saying that he was desperate to have children. He really wanted children. I kept on saying that I did not want another child yet. I had Sophie, who was at school and out of the toddler stage, I had my studies and I was busy. But he went on and on.

I was on the pill, and he started saying things like,

"You know, Lauren, since you've been on the pill, you've changed. You've become more emotional, and I don't think you're that same happy person you once were."

Which bothered me a bit, but I wasn't so convinced about. He was also voicing the same concerns to others, who would say to me,

"You know, Rob's worried about you, and I think he might be right, perhaps you can change it."

And I'd respond, "Back off! Leave it out, I'm fine!" Of course, this just made them all look at me and go,

"Right!"

As a result of the constant nagging, I was becoming irritable, the very thing he had described. So I went to the doctor's and changed the pill, but the same comments were coming back at me. This time from Sophie saying,

"Mummy, you seem more grumpy."

I went back to the doctor's, and the only solution was the mini-pill. So I switched to that, and of course, I fell pregnant. Much later, when I was dealing with the aftermath of his abuse of my daughters during a support group at Mosac, another mother of an abused child said that the very same thing had happened to her. I was horrified that in a room of only seven women, that two of us had been persuaded to change our normal birth control by a child sex offender.

With the pregnancy came that feeling again. Not about the pregnancy, but I had this gnawing feeling about him. It was so hard, I was really struggling with this feeling that I just did not like him at some level, and here I was pregnant with his child. I had nothing to go on, no reason for these feelings to be there. I didn't really know what to do, but I felt it was morally the right thing to tell him that I was expecting. Big mistake. I'd asked him not to tell anyone for a while, so we could consider the situation but he didn't do as he promised. He told lots of people, including his family who turned up with flowers. So that was that. I felt angry with him, but I couldn't go anywhere with it as he was so happy. He got everyone involved. How can you explain to people that it was so wrong of him to do that? How can you express your anger at your partner for simply telling everyone that he's thrilled at the prospect of having a baby? Most women would have chewed my arm off for such a man. I was all alone with these deep concerns. I couldn't tell anyone. I also came to the conclusion that I was on this path, and I just had to get on with it.

Throughout the pregnancy he was there all the time, watching over me. What I ate, the coffee I drank, what I did. All in a very caring but very controlling way. To the outside world he looked like he was being super supportive, but it was a bit oppressive. He was starting to put doubts in my mind about my parenting skills. Nothing big or dramatic, but he'd say things like,

"I don't think that you're doing enough for Sophie. I don't think you're dressing her well, perhaps she needs some new clothes."

We were poor, we all made do, but he really hurt me when he made comments like that. I'd get quite upset.

Some things never quite made sense with him, but he was so good at making things fit. He had two degrees, and was a really clever man, yet he worked as an engineer in a manufacturing company. At the time, there was a lot in the press about bigger corporations squeezing out the smaller ones. I asked him one day why someone so over qualified was working as he was. He told me that he'd had his own business, but that it had gone under because of a corporate giant not paying their bills on time. I just thought, 'you poor man.' Rob was a victim, and this was also borne out by his parents and I trusted his parents.

When I was heavily pregnant, around eight months, I had given up all my jobs as I was in my last year of university and I wanted to get things straight with my studies. Rob was going to take over the financial responsibility of the home. I'd saved some money to buy things for the baby - everything I had saved had gone into preparing for my baby to be born. I was really happy, and I was proudly showing all the things I'd bought to people.

He came home and I was showing him, and he said,

"Oh. You spent the money."

"Well, yes, we needed a cot, a pram, bottles etc, the list goes on!"

"Well, I wasn't expecting you to spend it," he replied.

"Yes, the money was for the baby, we talked about it." I was feeling lost.

"I don't have any money."

"What?"

LAUREN'S STORY

"I'm in debt, and I don't have any money. I thought the money was to pay the bills."

"Sorry?"

"There's no money."

And that was the situation I was in. All the money he earned went on clearing his debts. Not debts that he'd accrued because of his business failure, but because actually he was a heavy drinker and owed people all over the place. I'd had no idea and now I had no job. No money in the bank. Nothing.

He went off to work, and I picked up the phone and told his mum that we would need some money for food and that he was in debt. I was very polite and very sweet. His parents came around with a load of shopping. He went mental. Absolutely mental.

There was no pretence after that that he was nice. There was no pretence he liked me. From that moment on he behaved like I was a pile of shit. Oh the gloves were off then. He drank like a fish in my house, and it didn't matter what I told him, about Sophie being there, anything. The dope then came out, and I went mad. I didn't want it anywhere in the house, but he just taunted me saying that it'd been in the house for ages and it was just I hadn't noticed.

LAUREN'S STORY

I think he underestimated me at the time. I am a nice person, a sweet person, and he knew that he was able to twist me into accepting him in my life. I come across as such, but he never saw the fiery side of me. He undervalued my skills, and he should not have done. I think he thought I would be absolutely controlled at that point. I was heavily pregnant and there was no turning back so I think he thought he was on safe ground.

It was all down to me, again. I had to go out and find myself a job, which I did. Nearly eight months pregnant and starting another job. It was so stressful. A new job with all this going on, him drinking and smoking pot. I didn't drink or do drugs and I was very naive, I simply didn't know what to do. I would try and speak to him, but all he'd say was,

"Get rid of me then."

He would also blame me for his drinking, saying that I was awful to live with and making me feel really bad. Why was he there? If it was so awful, I was so awful, then go.

"I'm not going anywhere," he'd say.

When Jessica was born Rob turned quite nice again, he wasn't particularly helpful, but he was being pleasant. I had terrible flu after she was born, and I'd lost a lot of blood, and my caesarian scar ripped every time I sneezed. It was awful. I was in bed, and he came up and said,

"I'll make you some warm milk," and he came back upstairs with some hot chocolate, and I thought, 'ah that's so sweet'. I sat up and drank this in bed, and when I got to the bottom of the mug, I saw all this sludgy stuff.

"What's this?" I asked,

"Cannabis", he replied.

Oh shit. I suffered. I tried to vomit it back up, but it's a powerful anti-emetic, so I could not. Twenty minutes later, my heart rate had slowed right down. I was anaemic and I had the flu. He had slowed me right down, and I really thought I was going to die. I tried to call an ambulance, but he ripped the phone from my hand, and then I just slipped into a sleep. Why did he do that? Why did he need me to be passed out? What did he do when I was rendered unconscious? It still fills me with horror. I said to my neighbour that I was really scared and wanted him out of the house, and she said,

"Well. It was only cannabis, and you were having trouble sleeping, and you did sleep. He said he was trying to help you, and you did sleep."

No one wanted to listen or believe that he was being awful and doing awful things. He would not go. He told me he had squatter's rights, so I would have to make him go. I checked it out, and he was right. I was the owner and he wasn't paying any rent, and we had no contract. It would have taken me six months to evict him, and I'd still have to live with him, how bad would that be? I kept praying that he would just eventually go.

In all that time he had been courting me, working on me, I never knew what he was really like. He never showed himself other than a very sweet, warm person who couldn't do enough for me or Sophie. He was Mr Nice and everyone loved him - his friends, my family, my daughter, and eventually me. And when he needn't be nice to me anymore, he still maintained the act to everyone else. His friends, my family took his side when I wanted him to leave. He would also succeed in what I think would be his original aim, to befriend and entrance my daughter Sophie, and our daughter, Jessica, eventually sexually abusing them both.

Lauren paints a very clear picture of how she was taken in by Rob. How he not only charmed her, but her close network of family and friends. She also trusted his parents, who were respectable people in positions of trust.

I notice that she didn't really know much about his circle of friends, with much of the story centering on her world. This is also common with child sex offenders preying on women; they make the centre of their world the target family. At one level, it can be very alluring, flattering.

Rob was very skilled in entrapping Lauren, and it took some fight for her to be rid of him from her house. Lauren shares the story of how she was successful in making him leave the home - eventually. In doing so, she also shows more of the cruel, sinister side of him, revealed only when he had secured what he wanted from Lauren. She is certain that he never cared about her, and that his true feelings were revealed after Jessica was born. This is also consistent with the two faces of a child sex offender - the friend and the abuser.

He told lies to my family and friends about me. The worst was that I was having an affair, which meant that my family and friends were treating me really badly, and it's so hard to prove you're not having an affair. All the time it was "Poor Rob," and "that bitch Lauren." Still, he wouldn't leave. I had been advised by AA to stop clearing his debts, in order to halt funding for his continued drinking. It gave me some power back in the short term, but he used it to his advantage.

I came home one afternoon from work, finding out he'd taken the children out from the child minder. I walked in to find Sophie sitting there, rigid, on the sofa, and Jessica wailing from upstairs. He was upstairs in bed, passed out. There was debris around him, an empty bottle of vodka and the remains of a candle on the table, which had burnt through leaving the table glowing, smouldering. There was smoke everywhere. Sophie cried out to me,

"Mummy, Mummy. He told me to stay here. He told me to stay on the couch. I wanted to go to Jessica, but he wouldn't let me."

Jessica was screaming and screaming. She was purple when I got to her. I picked her up, and tried to soothe her, and went back into the bedroom to try and snuff out the embers on my table. I looked at him, slumped on the bed, and felt nothing but utter revulsion. Disgusted that he could get so pissed when he had the children. Why take the children out of the child minders, if he was going to get so pissed? That was it as far as I was concerned. He had put my children in danger, and I felt repulsed by him.

LAUREN'S STORY

I was trying to calm my children down, but all the time I was seething. There was also something bothering me about him, how he was. So I asked Sophie to hold Jessica and went back upstairs. I found boxes of pills, very dramatically left around, staged I believe. How many he had taken I don't know, but if he'd taken all that had been popped out, he would be dead. Even so, I immediately began to feel guilty for my previous feelings. I called an ambulance, and they took him in and pumped him out. He recovered pretty quickly. On a human level, I responded to him. What else could I have done? Of course his family and friends came to see him, crying,

"Why have you done this?"

"Because of Lauren. She's so mean to me. She hates me. I couldn't bear to go on anymore. I wanted to be with the children when I went because I love them so much. She's hurt me so much. She's having an affair. She won't help me pay my debts, I spent the money on her and the children"

This tale of woe spouted from his mouth, and they blamed me. The lies that came out of that man. I had apparently tipped him over the edge. The disgust soon came back to me. There were so many people having a go at me. His parents. My parents. My friends. All blaming me. I was trapped, totally trapped by this man. I cannot

begin to tell you how isolated I was, and how frightened I
was. I even went to see a solicitor to get some advice,
telling him I thought this man was a danger to my
children. No one listened to a fucking word I said.

I was the evil one, having an affair, and he was
depressed. No one listened to how I felt. Absolutely no
one. He had cut me off from everything, and I was under
huge pressure to take him back after this incident. I kept
asking him to go, but he refused. I'd say to him,

"If it's so bad here, if I am such a bitch to you, then
just go."

"I'm not going anywhere", he said.

Then he started to offer me an 'out clause' when he
began to add,

"I'll only leave when I know for sure you're having
an affair."

I didn't think much of this at the time, but it came
into play later.

It was the most extraordinary situation, that I was tied to
this man whom I now despised, held there by his own will
and supported by those around us. He played the victim so
well to those that came around us, and no one saw the
reality of it.

LAUREN'S STORY

The thing that was the final straw for me was when he showed me his knives. A family moved down the road who were notorious for bringing trouble, and Rob's response was to move his knives in. He showed me this great big box one day, and I said,

"What's that?"

"It's a box of knives, a strong box."

"Well, I don't want them here. I'm not interested. Take them away."

"We need protecting from that lot down the road, and they're staying. I'll show you."

I was sitting on the couch, and he proceeded to show me them. He undid this box, and I was stupefied by what I saw. I was rooted to the spot, they shocked me so much. I'm not talking about big kitchen knives, but specialist knives. Cutthroats. Scary kind of hunting knives, huge, with serrated edges and proper curved handles. He grabbed me, turned me round, and showed me how to use a cutthroat, telling me to slice from ear to ear so that I would be sure to cut the jugular. I had lost the power of speech. I was so frightened. I didn't know what to do next, but I was certain that I was being shown how I might die. I felt it was not a game, and he was showing me what he could do. He then turned me round, and switched to one with a serrated blade.

"With this one, what you do is shove it right into the belly and pull it up through the rib-cage. All the way up. Dragging it up with the serrations, so that you cut up the flesh. You can put your hand up the hole you've made and get to the heart."

I pulled myself away, and said,

"Put it away, now."

He just laughed.

I made his parents come and collect the box, which they did. That was a waste of time, because it made its way back into the house at some point. I didn't know what to do about him. I was terrified. What could I do with someone who has staged an overdose and turned everyone against me? Could I throw him out, when he's shown me his knives and he knows how to use them? I was so confused by him. I had begged his mother to take him away, trying to play the 'if it's so bad, if I'm so bad, then rescue him' card. It didn't work, as she believed he was better to be with his daughter.

How had I ended up in this mess? I had changed from being the girlfriend of a highly educated 'nice guy' with a devoted Christian family, to being trapped by a dangerous, manipulative alcoholic with a specialist knife box.

LAUREN'S STORY

I was so bitter inside, and I had no where else to go, so desperate to get rid of him. I knew he had to go and that I had to force the situation. I really wanted this situation to end. I had come to the point where I realised that no matter what I did, it was twisted and used against me. If I behaved myself and complied, all manner of horrors were coming my way. If I didn't behave myself, all manner of horrors were coming my way. So, I decided to give him what he wanted, to be a victim, to see if I could make him go. I remembered the 'out clause' he had given me and for my children's sake I was prepared to take any shit to resolve this quickly. I went out on a couple of dates with a bloke, nothing much happened, but it was very public. How stupid was I to do that? Perhaps I should have figured out by now that I wouldn't see what would come next. He had everything planned and he knew a fundamental rule about people, keep pushing someone and they will react eventually. Then he could use their reaction against them. Looking back I realise it was so stupid, I didn't mind that people thought I was a bitch - they did anyway - but it was stupid because it helped him gain support for the next part of his plan.

He actually didn't say anything to me. If anything he was slightly nicer. I was so shocked. No dramatics, nothing much happened at all. I was pretty annoyed at him to be honest. But it all unravelled pretty quickly.

Lauren is no longer the target of Rob's deception at this point, but he is still using manipulation of her friends and family to create the image of her that he wants them to have - a cheating, evil bitch. He has set her up, and used her own actions to create exactly the picture he wanted. Lauren has completely fallen victim to him. Rob has Lauren exactly where he wants her to be, and therefore his focus has shifted, from mother to daughters. Lauren is yet to discover that the fight is now over her daughter, Jessica. The battle begins on an inauspicious day when Lauren is returning from work to collect her daughters from the child minder's. Only, again, they are not there, and Lauren returns to the house with that sinking feeling.

I was shaking as I ran up the steps to the house, thinking perhaps he'd 'tried' to top himself again. I opened the front door and the whole house was trashed. Things turned over, drawers pulled out. I shouted for the kids, but there was no reply. They weren't there. I had no idea what was going on. My heart stood still as I just gawped at this mess. Then his parents turned up, so they must have been watching me down the road, and they came in with Sophie.

"Here's Sophie. Rob's got Jessica, and you'll be hearing from a solicitor..." and they just turned around and went.

I was completely dumbstruck. Sophie was in floods of tears. I went round the house and realised that he'd taken everything of Jessica's. I was walking from room to room realising that he had done this to my home. He had trashed my house. My first instinct was to go and fetch her back, but I also thought that if I did that, he'd have social services around saying I wasn't a suitable mother and they'd walk straight in to see this horrendous mess. He'd done this deliberately. It was vile. He had slowed me down because he knew I had to clear it up. I actually called the police, and they told me that it was a 'technical kidnap' because we weren't married, but they felt because he was the father, he had rights to look after her. I tried telling them he was a danger to her, but all they said was that if they went to collect her, she'd end up in care while we slugged it out in the family court. 'Thanks', I thought. I was on my own. I stayed up all night cleaning up, and I managed to make it better.

LAUREN'S STORY

Then there was this question of me finding her. Where was she? I had Sophie too, but whom could I trust to mind her when I was looking for Jessica? I phoned my solicitor and he told me much the same thing - that we'd have to go to court to get her back, which could take several months. I was aghast. This fiery part of me then kicked in, the mother who was going to protect her children. When his vile actions had been aimed at me I was weak but no one messes with me when it comes to my children. I got a friend to stay with Sophie, and I went off looking - all the places where I thought he might be hanging out. I actually found him quite quickly, but he was surrounded by his friends. I had to think really carefully, so I went back home to work out how I might deal with this. There was a voice inside me going 'he will not cope - at some point he is going to leave her...' That was my hope. He would end up leaving her, probably with his parents, and that would be the time for me to act. I had to go into work each day as if nothing was going on, all calmly, so I had to watch and wait in the evenings when Sophie was being looked after by my friend.

I was at work when I received a call from a solicitor, saying,

"I have Mr F in my office, and he wants to speak to you."

"Put him on", I replied as casually as I could.

LAUREN'S STORY

"I have a consent order drawn up for me to have sole custody of Jessica, and you're going to sign it or you'll never see her again!"

So much for only women doing this! I simply said,

"I don't think so. I know who you are now, and I have a picture of it. I am going to do what I need to do to get her back, and it's going to be so quick you will not know what happened to you..." I put the phone down.

I wasn't nasty, just firm. This wonderful strong mother in me going 'you will not get away with this and you will not harm my beautiful child.' Almost immediately afterwards I received a call from the CSA[10], saying that 'Mr F' had put in a claim six months previously for support of Jessica. This was before the 'suicide attempt,' before even I'd decided the relationship was over. He had been plotting this, building up to this point. His solicitor had simply nudged the CSA. I felt completely isolated, and quite scared. I can't pretend that I was all fire but it was the fire to get my daughter back that drove me onwards. I kept up the vigil, and sure enough, within a matter of days he'd left her alone.

---

[10] The CSA, or Child Support Agency, is a statutory agency in the UK whose role is to make sure that parents who live apart from their children contribute financially to their upkeep by paying child maintenance.

171

LAUREN'S STORY

Jessica had been left at Rob's parents', of course, so that he could go off with his mates and get pissed. I waited for about twenty minutes in case he was coming back, and marched up to the front door, armed with knowledge of the law. We weren't married even though his name was on the birth certificate as the father, this was kidnap and he wasn't with her. His mum answered the door and I said,

"I've come to take Jessica back. She's been kidnapped, and you've aided and abetted. If we go to the police, they will put her into care. You can choose whether that happens, or you can hand her back to me, her mother. Your son is not capable of looking after her, and you know it."

After some discussion, they handed her over. I walked away joyous, thinking 'fucking hell.' I really didn't think they'd part with her. Jessica was 18 months, something like that. She says she remembers it, being so relieved that I had come for her. It had been four or five days before he had left her alone, and it was just awful. It was like she had been ripped out of my life. She had gone, with her cot, covers, toys, everything. It was just horrid. I cannot begin to express the pain of her not being there. It was just horrid.

I had made a kind of deal with Rob's parents in securing Jessica from them. They had realised that it wasn't in anyone's interests for her to be the subject of an emergency care order, which is why they handed her back, but they also were looking to protect the interests of their son. I agreed that we would go to the family court. I negotiated with them and in court, we made an agreement for supervised access and thus parental responsibility would be automatically given but only if Jessica stayed permanently in my care. I wanted Jessica back without any fear of losing her again and felt that if supervised access took place, then Rob would be less likely to have reason to take her again. I also saw the emotional difficulties Sophie had experienced from her father's disappearance and I didn't want Jessica to suffer in this way. I felt at the time that I was doing the best in a bad situation.

Lauren had her own family back together, and from this day onwards, life for Jessica would be divided between her two families. For several years, life settled down to a pattern of visits in accordance with the court order of the family court. Lauren thought that things were going well, and that she was largely free from the torment of the man that had slipped so easily into her life.

THE YEARS ROLL BY

Lauren tells me that she has two histories. She has had to recast her life for the things she found out in retrospect. The life that she lived forwards no longer exists - it had to be edited for the events which happened, and she found out about much later. It was not easy for her to rewrite - not only was it painful to put in some of the details, but it was complicated. The realities were not delivered in a neat, seamless way by her daughters, but fragments were given to Lauren here and there, and she was ceaselessly going over the past, piecing this story together. The editing is not finished to this day, as more revelations emerge. The story that I have crafted from Lauren attempts to give the stories side by side, the life she lives forward, with intersections of the reality of life with Rob.

Despite my reservations, the access seemed to go really well. There were no more dramas or incidents, and Rob stuck to the agreement of the court order. His parents also persuaded me that he had taken treatment for his drinking and that he was sober now. There was one occasion when I got really worried about Jessica, but the problem was sorted out, so you think that everything is all right. The routine was that his parents would pick her up from the child-minder on the Friday for weekend access. There was this one weekend when Jessica came back she was very sore - not nappy rash sore, but inside more. I understood that the only time when this happens is when a child is left in a pooey nappy for too long, where bacteria starts to infect the aggravated skin. I phoned his parents to see what they had noticed, and they put Rob on the phone too. I asked them if they had noticed the soreness, and they said that it was like it when they picked her up from the child minder's. I told them I was going to go to the doctor's, as I was worried about her, as she was also burning up. Rob insisted on coming with me. It turns out that it was a bladder infection that had caused the problems, which I was confused about. I was placated by the doctor and took her out of that child minder. It didn't happen again, so that was that issue dealt with.

Do you know the truth? This is one of the examples of things you re-examine. It wasn't a pooey nappy that caused the bladder infection. There are things I look back on and I am just horrified, and this is one of them. It was him, his actions, molestations that caused it. Girls getting bladder infections at that age is really unusual, it is cause for alarm - so I now understand. I went to the doctor, concerned but not knowing why, and my concerns were explained away, taking me away from my own instinct of being alarmed, my own good sense pushed aside by the reasoning of the doctor and Rob. It didn't happen again, so that was the problem gone. Forgotten about for many years.

Yes, the access went well for years. Then in the last few years, Rob asked for an extension of access, wanting to become more involved in the access arrangements. I referred back to my solicitor, as it was not what I really wanted, but because there had been no problems over the years it was hard for me to object to his requests. I could object as much as I wanted in private, but without good reason the courts would not hear me. I was told that I would be seen as 'acrimonious' if I tried to prevent this extension. I was uncomfortable about the increased independence in his access, which would involve him picking Jessica up from school on a Friday, but I had to go along with it. The courts had in effect silenced my concerns.

Nothing happened to alarm me for some time. My concerns seemed to be proved wrong. Rob then applied to take Jessica for a two-week holiday with his parents. My feelings were all over the place about it, but I had no logical reason to prevent this happening. Jessica wanted to go with her daddy, and so that was that. She seemed to be settled - she did well at school, was well liked. She would sometimes be traumatised at night, but I put that down to the fact that we had recently moved house and she said she hated her new room. Sometimes she would come back a bit grumpy from her dad's, but as it was a difficult situation for a child to cope with, the emotional adjustment, I made allowances. She would also be very tired at times, but I figured it was all to do with the adjustments of being in two homes. She never complained about her father and I was comforted by the thought that she was safe with her grandparents there.

I was very aware that Sophie was not part of this arrangement, and at times I wished she had her dad to take her out, so when Jessica went to her dad's, I'd make 'us' time for Sophie and me, which we both really enjoyed. I think sometimes Jessica missed her big sister, so when Jessica wanted to take Sophie out for a birthday treat with her dad, it meant everything to her to be allowed to do it. Jessica loved it, being out with her sister and her other family, and a part of me was really happy that Sophie was being included. This became a pattern that they would take Sophie out on her birthday. In 2004, Sophie and Jessica came back from the birthday outing really excited.

"I've been invited on the family holiday, and I'm thrilled, and Jessica's so excited - can I go? Can I go? Can I go?"

My initial reaction was to scream at her "Noooooooooo!" I was not happy about the holiday, and I said to her,

"But why now? You're 14, why now?"

I don't know what I thought, that she might be used as a free babysitter, that they wouldn't treat her well, that she'd be left out... many things. Her reply really threw me, she screamed at me,

"I knew you'd be like this. They said you'd be like this, that you don't want me to go, that you'd put your feelings first and be difficult...."

It smelt like lines of his emotional blackmailing that I'd heard all those years ago, and I did not like it one bit. But what could I do? She was so excited about it, as was Jessica. I couldn't think about it very clearly, so I checked it out with a couple of friends, who basically said what could go wrong with his parents and Jessica there? How could I deny them this excitement? It also had struck me that this would be a holiday when they would be together, which rarely happened on holidays. Normally, Jessica would be off with his family, and I'd pay for Sophie to go with a friend of hers and her family. I couldn't afford a holiday for all of us. This would be an opportunity for them to be together, so this made it more of a good opportunity. All of this together made for no real reason for me to say no. Other than I felt uncomfortable about it on some level. I even checked it out with his parents - the girls would be in one room, and the boys in the other. That was that. In the summer of 2004, they went away together.

It was really tough for me when they were away, and I was nervous waiting for their arrival back home. Jessica was the one who returned a little distressed from this holiday, but getting to the bottom of it was a complete minefield. She'd said that she'd had sunstroke, and that she'd been unwell and that her dad had given her bottled water to take, but she didn't like the taste of it. She was adamant that it was bought water, and that the water had made her feel sick, but her dad was insistent that she drank it. I could not fathom what was going on. She had said that the doctor had visited her, and she spoke about her grandparents, so I was reassured that they had been caring for her, and I didn't want to push her. If she was poorly, she could have been delirious, so I just let it go about the water. I checked with his parents, and they said she was ill with sunstroke, and blamed it on her not wearing a hat when she should. So that was that. There was also something else she said which disturbed me, because it was so odd. She was also saying that when her daddy came to put her to bed and said goodnight, he wouldn't let her sleep with her knickers on, because she was too hot. Now, she never wears knickers at night at home, just pyjamas. I asked her why it was so important to wear knickers on holiday,

"Well, because he's a boy and I'm a girl," she replied, emphatically.

I guessed she was becoming more self-aware, and at the age of seven, she's decided that she's keeping herself private from her daddy because he's a boy. As if to prove the point, from this day onwards, she wore her knickers at night.

What really happened on that holiday? Like me, you may already be filling in some of the possibilities. It is almost easy, but then you and I have the context in which this story is presented - a book about the parents of children who have been sexually abused. The reality is beyond what Lauren feared at the time, concerned for Rob's drinking and drug taking past and the neglect of her children under those circumstances. Would they be safe in his care? The reality is not.

Lauren has now pieced together what really went on during that family holiday to Greece. It is shocking - the acts committed against Rob's own daughter, and her sister. Lauren recounts to me what she subsequently found out.

The holiday to Greece? I had every reason to be worried about it, I was so fearful about it. Deep inside I knew that it wasn't safe, but I let myself be persuaded otherwise, by him, his parents and my own friends. I had no contrary evidence to go on anyway. Everyone said I was being over sensitive. It turns out that his parents were not there all the time, and when they were, they were in a completely different hotel. I'd been lied to by the people I had really trusted in all this. Rob had secured a family room, which they all shared together. His parents had been there when Jessica was ill with sunstroke, but not all the time. They had enough experience to pacify me afterwards. Why do they cover for him? It completely mystifies me. Why on earth did they keep lying for him? I was so taken in by them. The water that he was making her drink was vodka, so no wonder she didn't like the taste. God! He gave her vodka! What an evil, twisted man. He gave them both vodka - so that they'd pass out. He raped my daughter Sophie in that hotel room. He got them drunk so that he could have sex with her. How do I know this? Because he hadn't given Jessica quite enough, and she saw what he did to her sister. She was so terrified that it would be her next that she insisted on keeping her knickers on. That's why she still wears them, to protect herself. I wish with all my heart I could go back and stop that holiday from taking place. He also took Sophie to get some weird piercings, but that's a whole other story.

After their holiday life returned back to normal quickly enough, and the pattern of access resumed. Sophie was getting more invites to access visits, and increasingly she wanted to go along. Jessica seemed pleased that her sister was involved, so I went along with it. It was all going very well, really. Sophie was struggling a lot at school with her science, and she was getting into a complete panic about a science test. She had worked herself into a state that she was so bad at science. Rob was really good at science - it was one of his degrees and he'd tutored a girl before when he was living with me - so he offered to do the same for Sophie. Give her some private tuition to get her through this test. I was working full-time, but worked from home at times, so I said that he could tutor her on those occasions when I was at home, which they both were in agreement with. However Jessica was also around, and they said that she was bothering them, so he took Sophie off to the library. He gave her five of these tutorials, and on three of them, they took off to the library. I couldn't find anything to refute the logic of going there, so they went. Anyway, Sophie got a very bad science test result, so I was able to say, "That's that", and put a stop to these sessions. They never went to the library of course, just off somewhere together. Sneaking around.

I also learned later that he would go and collect Sophie from my mum's. If I was having to work late, or was away on business, the girls would go to my mum's. Only he was collecting Sophie on some occasions and telling Mum that it was OK with me, so she would just let her go. My mum never questioned it, or never thought to tell me about it.

All these occasions when I really had no idea what was happening. I still find that so very hard to cope with. You think you know what's going on. You think you know where they are. You think you know who they're with. You think they're safe. And they're not. I find it so hard to cope with. It eats away at you. You thought you knew, but you knew nothing.

When you live Lauren's life forwards, suspending the fact that you know the context for her story, it reads like many families in the situation of trying to navigate access and ensuring that the children are put first. It is not unreasonable for an absent parent to holiday with their children. This was even my situation growing up. My sister and I lived with our mum after our parents separated, and our dad took us out for trips, and also on holiday. It is very normal. I imagine that our mum had her own reservations and anxieties, which is also normal and natural, and it is also normal for friends to persuade you that you're being neurotic. My sister and I used to look forward to time with our dad. When all parties appear to be happy, then why would you do anything differently? Sophie went away with Jessica's 'other family' the following year, because the first vacation together was successful. Rob was again being so nice, so reliable, so accommodating. Lauren was persuaded that he was behaving as a dad should, so when he suggested he changed the way he provided his maintenance support, she listened to him.

LAUREN'S STORY

I was in a period of work when I had to travel a lot more, and I had to pay more in childcare costs to cover this. My days were longer at times because I was on the road more. Rob was paying a small amount in maintenance, not much, and the child minding costs were crippling me. He offered to come over and do some of the extra babysitting duties in return for halting this small amount of maintenance. To be honest, I didn't think that long about it. Sophie had been away a couple of times with him, and seemed to get along with him, so it was more of a "why not?" It was a solution, and would only be a few times a month, so I agreed.

My God, looking back do I regret that easy decision. I find it so hard to cope with now. How I just opened the door to him, back into my life, my family life. I was lulled by him so much. I have painted a picture of this man who was so charming, and then so evil, so vile and I was desperate to get him out of my home. When did I forget that bit? For eight years he goes into 'nice daddy' mode, and everyone, myself included, thinks he's great with the kids, always on time, always sticking with the arrangements. I was so taken in with this caring side of him, again! When I look back and recount the vile things he did to me, and I let him take care of my children to save

185

a few pounds spent on childcare costs. It is so hard to contend with, so hard to reconcile. I'm not sure how I can ever get over that.

The truth is that Rob was adept at deception and manipulation, a toolkit possessed by most child sex offenders. When there is deception and collusion played out by her daughters, those complex layers are almost impossible to uncover. Lauren had experienced both sides of Rob, 'Mr Nice' and 'Mr Nasty'. I imagine that at one level, Lauren wanted to believe that Rob was 'Mr Nice' when it came to their child, Jessica, and her other daughter, Sophie. The mind has a remarkable way of steering things towards its own preference. At the same time, it is easy for me to look in and notice patterns about things, and cross-reference them to my own understanding of how child sex offenders operate. It may also seem obvious to you, as a reader. What is surprising is what happened next, which triggered the chain of events that ultimately led to the revelation of the ordeal to which her daughters had been subjected.

ANOTHER REALITY

The whole thing blew up when I had to attend an awards dinner in London. The product that I was responsible for had won an award, so it was supposed to be an evening when I shone. However I just didn't want to be there, I had this horrible feeling inside me, and all I knew was that I wanted to be home. I don't drink much, and I can't bear wine, so I was on water, and this event seemed to be dragging on and on. As soon as the presentations were over, I slipped away early, taking a cab home.

I came through the front door and into the living room. I must've been pretty quiet as he was just sitting there on the floor in front of the TV. As soon as I walked in, I knew he was pissed, very drunk, and he was smoking a spliff. I sat down and said,

"You're going to have to go."

He said to me, "You've been drinking, haven't you?"

"Did you hear what I just said, you've got to go," I replied.

He got up casually and said,

"I'll make you a cup of coffee," and he went into the kitchen to make me this coffee.

It was then I noticed his bag stuffed under the couch, full of bottles and beer cans. I thought to myself, 'Oh my God! If he's had this much to drink, and is getting up and making me coffee, and functioning, this is a serious drink problem.' My stomach just lurched, and the reality of it swam around me. He must have been drinking that much every fucking day, for years. Shit. My whole world came to pieces in that one moment. How much of an idiot am I? However, I girded myself, and calmly said to him,

"Just drink your coffee, and then you've got to go."

"I'll go when I'm good and ready."

He just sat there and drank his coffee, making no effort to move. He just sat there as cool as cucumber. It was like being thrown back in time. Another realisation hit me and I said to him,

"You're not working are you?"

"You know I'm not working," he replied.

"How long?"

Then he just launched into this tirade of abuse. Telling me that I was a bad, negligent mother, and that all I gave a shit about was work, that I should not be drinking, and because I had been, he could not leave. Here he was again, turning reality upside down. I hadn't been drinking so I ignored that part. I said,

"Well, you go out to work, and earn enough to cover this, and I will gladly stay at home with the children. It will be a gift from God."

LAUREN'S STORY

I had reached that point, *again*, where I'd had enough, and it was 'bang', right, you need to go now, so I turned to him and said,

"Look, this conversation is over, and you need to leave my home, right now."

He was completely ignoring me, looking through me. So I stood in front of the TV, and leaned in towards him, and said,

"You are going to have to go."

I said it exactly like that, calmly. He reached up his hand, and grabbed my throat, and pulled me down. He wasn't throttling me like you see on films with both hands. He was very casual about it; he still had the spliff in the other hand, and one hand with his fingers behind my windpipe, squeezing really hard. I was on the floor, and I had this moment of shock - is this happening? - and then it was, 'I am not going to die on this floor and leave this man with my children.' Something inside me kicked in, and I reacted. I am so proud of myself, to this day, that I fought back. I took the opportunity to fight back and shocked him as he had shocked me. I literally pulled his hair and put my weight on his hair and his head to try and pull myself up. I caught his breath. I dug my nails in, and he let go. You could see the shock in his face, that I had the strength to fight him. He had let go, so I slid myself away trying to scream at him to get out but my voice wouldn't work properly. He was so calm. I have no idea what was going through his head, but he slowly put his shoes on and made his way out of the front door. I could hear him fiddling with the latch on the porch door, so I didn't know what to do. Was he latching it so that he could come back? I started to dial the police, but I didn't really want the same reaction from them as last time, so when I knew he had gone, I put the phone down and checked the porch door. It wouldn't lock. I bolted the inner door securely and watched in case he tried to return.

I was stunned listening to this account, but it was the way that the attack was so calm and somehow sinister that chilled me. I knew that Lauren was recounting the attack with absolute accuracy because her body told the same story: she was trembling as she relived it for me; her voice wavered when she recalled how proud she was of herself in that moment for fighting back; and, she was coughing and spluttering as she spoke of being throttled, like her body was remembering the sensation of being strangled.

Lauren has every right to be proud of herself for fighting back, it would prove to be pivotal in her story - not only in seeing Rob for what he really was, but also in bringing her into contact with a sympathetic police officer (Rob later alleged she had attacked him and she had to go to the police) who would be the first witness to her daughter's story of sexual abuse.

Having suffered this brutal attack, Lauren was at a loss as to what to do next.

What did I do? Would the police aggravate him if I called them? Would they even bother to do anything? Did I have to see Rob again? Would it make things worse again? Ultimately, it was all about my kids and keeping them safe. When Sophie got up the next morning, she was expecting to see Rob there, and I had to explain to her that I wasn't going to my meeting, and that he wasn't coming over and that she and Jessica weren't going to ever be on their own with him again. She got really upset, which completely threw me. I was tired, sore, and I ended up just yelling at her,

"This is the way it is, he's drinking heavily again, and I'm trying to protect you!"

I went to see my doctor later that morning, as my hand was really swollen where I'd landed on the wooden floor, and I wanted him to take a note of my injuries on my throat. He advised me to go to the hospital to get my hand checked out, so I did, but it wasn't broken. Just very swollen. It was such a tough day, which got worse when Sophie came home.

"You attacked Rob. He's got blood in his hair, and nail marks on his face" she accused.

"No. He attacked me, and I defended myself, but let's not get into that."

The venom that came out of her was awful. It stopped me from thinking about how in the hell, and why, she had this story. What had he told her, and why?

I knew I had to sort access out again, but I also knew that the family court wouldn't just let me run to the court without trying to resolve things myself first. I had to show that I'd tried to negotiate. I tried to revert back to the first court order, but he would not agree. At this stage we were communicating by email, and I had this email from him saying that I had attacked him, stuff like, "I will pick up Jessica as normal and don't try to stop me," he was really threatening. I then noticed the 'cc' on the email. It was Adrian, Sophie's Dad! He'd come back into her life about a year before, and Adrian and Rob had wanted to meet to kind of see all of the adults involved in Sophie's life.

LAUREN'S STORY

I could not believe he was on this email, so I called Adrian up and said,

"Why are you copied in on this mail?"

"Well, you're doing to him what you did to me..."

"What!" I couldn't believe what I was hearing.

"Well, you were so awkward with me about Sophie when I came back, and now you're doing the same with him."

"What, because you left her like Garfield at the window, and I was cross with you? I didn't want you to do that to her again. Come on!"

"You probably won't let him see Sophie, so I will when she's over with me!"

Oh my God! Rob has convinced Adrian that he was hard done by. He was giving Adrian an out clause for his guilt in abandoning Sophie, by convincing him that I'm some absolute bitch, and now they're in cahoots together. I was furious.

"Right. Did you know that Rob drinks really heavily?"

"No."

"Do you want your daughter spending time with someone who drinks really heavily?

"No."

"Do you know that he also uses cannabis?"

LAUREN'S STORY

"No."

"If you're happy with that, and you act on it, I will be calling social services. Just stay out of this, Adrian. Tell Rob you're not going to be used in this manner."

I said all this to him, but I don't think it's where it ended with them at all.

I had to go back to the family court and make an emergency application, as he said that he was going to turn up at the school and collect Jessica. I couldn't face a scene at the school, so I kept Jessica out of school and made this application as well as a restraining order. They granted it, but only until the next contact order. Great, I was back in the courts. His solicitor was so aggressive, and I have this barrister - you often get a barrister that you've never met - but she was actually pretty good. I was given this statement to read. I didn't have much time to read it, and because of my dyslexia, I notice patterns in the writing. I remember things like there were seven paragraphs on page two, and the lengths of the paragraphs. Patterns and the amount of writing are very important to someone who can't follow words well. It wasn't signed. They had taken it into the court, unsigned. The judge commented on it, and his solicitor was apologising, saying that there was no time and it was their only copy.

LAUREN'S STORY

In this statement, they'd said that I'd attacked Rob, and that they'd referred the matter to the police, who were going to arrest me. I was horrified. This was potentially very damaging to my work. I worked in a senior position for a FTSE100 company in a security role. It was very bad news for me. It was dreadful. The point about this statement. Well, we never were given a copy at the time, we were told we would, but we never did. When a copy of it did eventually turn up it was a much longer statement and the story had changed - I know it was different. This was very difficult to prove, according to my barrister, and it was a very serious thing to accuse them of. My barrister agreed that she thought it had changed but we didn't have any evidence that it was different - no original copy was lodged with the court so I couldn't go anywhere with it. This underhand behaviour was just the start of the awful games and devious methods that would keep me spinning.

At the second court hearing, his solicitor requested that CAFCASS[11] be involved. I didn't know who CAFCASS were, but my barrister explained that they worked with the family court, and provided an independent view on the situation in the family. I agreed, thinking that they would

---

[11] CAFCASS looks after the interests of children involved in family proceedings in the UK. They have a role to work with children and their families, and then advise the courts on what they consider to be in the best interests of individual children.

be really helpful, and look at things in a practical way. How very naive was I?

The children obviously knew that I was going back to the courts, because there was a problem with access visits with Rob. I wanted to explain to Sophie about the second court order, the one that restricts Rob from driving the children, because I wanted her to understand that it was breaking the order for her to be driven by him. I thought she needed to know and understand that.

"Where's the other court order?" she spat at me. Her friend was standing there too, looking all snidely at me, her arms crossed.

"You want to see the first one, from all those years ago?" I questioned.

"Yes." Both now stood there with their arms crossed.

So, I went to hunt it out, and I found it and showed it to them. It's almost identical.

"Where's the court order that says he's not allowed to see me, and that he's only allowed to take me out once a year on my birthday?"

"There is no such court order. You were in the first order, as you can see, but Rob and his parents chose for you not to attend."

LAUREN'S STORY

She just burst into tears, and her friend's face dropped. He'd told her that I'd stopped her from having access together with Jessica and him for all those years. I wanted to know what else he had said. They told me that Rob had promised them that when they turned 16, he would get a house and that they could go and live there with him. The 'they' were Sophie and her two friends. They would be free to do whatever they wanted to. I couldn't believe what I was hearing. She also confessed to me about the piercings that she'd had done when they were in Greece, Rob had arranged for it, and paid for it. The piercings were all around her private areas, so I never knew about them. It was disgusting. Actually, I called the police about it at the time. We were unable to do anything about it - because it happened in Greece, and it was the person who performed the piercings that had committed the crime, not Rob.

The girls also asked if I had a bag of cans and bottles that Rob had left behind on the night of the attack. I said that I did have it. They told me that he had asked them to find the bag and give it back to him. Thankfully, I had locked the evidence in the boot of my car. It dawned on me that this is why he had broken the lock on the porch door on purpose so he could come back and get this bag. Sophie said that he had managed to get a copy of the key to the inside door but didn't have a porch door key. I changed the lock pronto.

From here on inwards, I would gather bits and pieces of things Rob had either said or done. This was all coming out between the police interviews, meetings with the courts and CAFCASS interviews. It was very confusing. I was expressing my worries to CAFCASS, who were completely ignoring them, because their primary access concern was with Jessica, Rob's daughter. I was getting really worried about Sophie, but CAFCASS just weren't interested.

I had ended up going to the police about the accusation of assault. Rob had claimed that I had attacked him, so I had no choice but to make a counter allegation with the police stating what really happened, that he had attacked me. I went down to the police station to give my version of events. The male officer who was dealing with my case reacted in the way I had dreaded. He made me feel that I wasn't worth any effort, just as they had made me feel before when I called them about Jessica's kidnap. They had allocated different police officers to deal with our complaints. The female officer dealing with Rob's few scratches on the other hand was very keen to arrest me. I couldn't understand how they could treat an attempted strangulation so blasé, but want to arrest me for scratching him. When I got to the police station, expecting to be arrested by the officer dealing with Rob's allegations, I was mistaken for my solicitor by the detective. God only knows what Rob had made me out to be, some kind of monster. I was so scared about being arrested, so I was relieved when they said that I wouldn't be arrested but that I would be interviewed instead. I'd prepared a document for my solicitor, bullet point form, so that she would be more prepared, and I also didn't trust myself not to recall everything, wrecked with nerves, shaking all over.

The police interview was completely surreal. The questions were all about me going out, and I really don't go out... Give an account of the evening... Did you talk about finances when you returned? How much do you drink - I don't drink, I don't like alcohol, I'll occasionally have a pint, but I hate wine... How often do you leave the children to go out with your boyfriend? What - I don't have a boyfriend... I have a doctor's note about my injuries... Then at the very end she said,

"Is there anything else you want to tell us?"

I told her that I was really worried about Sophie, and that CAFCASS were not listening to me, or prepared to speak to her. I told them about the piercings. The mood changed in the room, and she again asked me if there was anything else. My solicitor pointed to my bulleted list, and I told her about the kidnapping when Jessica was small and the whole business about that 'overdose'. She got up and said that she wanted to check some things out. I was so scared that they were going to arrest me. I was left in this police interview room for a couple of hours. It was gruesome.

When she came back, she confirmed that there was a record of my call about the piercings. She also confirmed that the child protection team had said that there was nothing we could do in respect of this, which we knew. She then turned to me and said,

"I am telling you, off the record, not to let your daughter or her friends anywhere near this man."

Thank you! This is exactly how I feel, and for the very first time I had experienced someone taking me seriously. She said I would hear from her, but that if I needed advice again, I could go to her. They basically NFA (No Further Action) the two allegations, and told us to go and sort it out in the family court.

Lauren's life had been turned completely upside down, and she describes the sensation of surrealism - that it was no

longer her life, and that things were almost happening around her. The central point was outside of her, and she felt like she was in a spin. There was an endless series of meetings - CAFCASS, the courts, solicitors, and the police - and she felt out of control of the situation. Lauren would not have a good experience with CAFCASS, and she is very open with her experiences. It evidently troubles her still, as her voice quickened with an air of exasperation. Not everyone who has to work with CAFCASS has such a trying experience, but at Mosac we often hear that CAFCASS are very slow and deliberate. They have a line to tread between both parents, and you hope for their objectivity. It does seem that in Lauren's case, the CAFCASS officer was swayed by Rob, the skilled charmer. Lauren explains her interactions with CAFCASS.

I found CAFCASS extremely unreasonable to deal with. Jessica was going in to be interviewed, and Sophie was getting really distressed. She really wanted to speak to someone in CAFCASS, but they just were not prepared to hear her. Jessica also started to act really oddly, and when we were going in, she asked me,

"Mummy, when I go in there, is there something you want me to say?"

"No, sweetie, this is for you to say how you feel, it's your time."

"Are you sure?"

"Absolutely."

Jessica went in for the interview, and when it had finished, the woman who had interviewed her came over to me and said,

"It took me nearly an hour to get anything out of that child." I was completely taken aback by her tone, it was so fierce.

"This is what she finally came out with," and she slammed a piece of paper down in front of me. On it was written:

I want to live with my Dad

In the tiniest letters, was written "Dad". I felt sick.

"She's so frightened, she can't even write Dad properly! She's so scared of your reaction to her. You told her that her dad was a drunk."

LAUREN'S STORY

"Err, no. No I did not. I told her that her dad could not pick her up because he'd had a drink that day and he could not drive. I never said he was a drunk."

I'd been more open with Sophie but not Jessica. I was careful how I worded things with her.

They absolutely attacked me. What had I done wrong? He has a history of drink and I have one of being reasonable. I have not interfered with access. I haven't bitched about him. I am only back here after eight years of scheduled access saying, "we have a major problem here." I have done nothing wrong in all of this. Why do you have this attitude towards me? I just didn't understand. They seemed to be ignoring the facts in front of them. He didn't have a job. He lived with his parents. He had a drink problem - he admitted it in his statement - along with the fact that he had a criminal record. He evidently couldn't look after himself, and it seemed that they were going to tell the court that Jessica could live with him. I did not know where to turn.

Sophie was still pleading with me to speak to CAFCASS herself, directly. She didn't want to talk to me about it, but really wanted someone from CAFCASS to hear her. I spoke to the woman that was dealing with us, and said,

"Can you speak to Sophie, please, she really wants to talk to you."

"No, I don't want to talk to her," was the reply.

"But the court order names both children, you have to."

"No. The court letter only refers to Jessica, as Sophie is old enough to make her own decisions."

They refused to speak to Sophie. I felt the inference was that I had put her up to making the request. Sophie wouldn't tell me about whatever it was, and CAFCASS wouldn't listen to me saying that I was very concerned about her. When I got back from the meeting, Sophie was in floods of tears at home, and so was Jessica. I was trying to console them both, but they were both so distressed. Jessica sobbed to me,

"Mummy, I've changed my mind, Daddy told me to say that I wanted to live with him, and I'm scared. I want to take it back."

"Don't worry; we'll sort it out,"

It was all I could say to both of them, although I had no idea how I would be able to pierce the impenetrable wall of CAFCASS. The next morning, I tried. I called up the same woman, and pleaded with her,

"My children are in a complete mess, and Jessica has told me that her dad told her what to say to you.

Sophie is in floods of tears about that, and distressed that you won't see her. I don't know what is going on, but I am really worried about my children. I need your advice."

She gave me the number of a family therapist whom I might try, so I called them up. I spoke to a very pleasant lady on the phone about what was going on, and they said they thought CAFCASS should speak to Sophie because it was a worrying case. They didn't want to confuse what was going on there, so told me to go back to CAFCASS. CAFCASS were not changing the way they responded to me. Access was going on, because it had to, and he was blatantly breaking the order by driving Jessica around. I was back with the solicitor writing letters to his solicitor complaining about these breaches. It was really winding me up. They clearly were not going to stick to the court order or agree to anything, so they forced me back into court. I honestly think that they thought I wouldn't raise the funds to go back into court, but I re-mortgaged my house, again, so that we could go back in front of the judge. I was running out of patience with CAFCASS.

I had contacted CAFCASS to tell them that Rob had shaved his hair, and bleached what remained of it. He was volunteering for a Tricho Test (a hair strand test for drugs), only had destroyed the evidence by removing his hair. The CAFCASS woman responded,

"Well, when he came to see me, his hair wasn't shaved off."

She would not listen to me telling her that there were witnesses who would attest to this - from the school, Jessica's teacher had been so shocked she had mentioned it to me. There were strong witnesses. I had nothing but unbelievable aggression from this one CAFCASS woman. It was like he was the poor little soul, and I was some awful alpha female. And of course, I'm now beginning to act like an alpha female because I was scared for my children and getting frustrated trying to get them to see clear evidence.

Sophie seemed to be at breaking point this one night, she kept crying and saying she needed to talk to someone, so I called up the police officer who had interviewed me over the assault, the one who told me to keep my children away from Rob. I said,

"I don't know where else to turn, the counselling service are saying it's too risky to speak to her, CAFCASS are telling me that they don't want to talk to her, and I do not know what to do, because she is getting so distressed. I am so very scared, and she won't tell me."

I put Sophie on the phone, and when asked what it was she wanted to talk about, she said,

"Just stuff..."

LAUREN'S STORY

The officer asked if she could come around, with a colleague, but Sophie didn't want me in the house. Of course, they couldn't agree to that, so Sophie conceded that it would be a private meeting, and that I would remain elsewhere in the house. They arrived a bit later, and went into the living room. Jessica was upstairs, so I was confined to the kitchen. I was clanking pans, trying to be noisy, so that I couldn't hear anything. I clanked around for what seemed like an eternity. I smoked a lot of fags in the garden. Then, the police officer appeared, and said,

"Can we please sit down?"

Those words. Can - we - please - sit - down? Horrendous.

Lauren and her children had been in this nightmare between courts, CAFCASS and the police over a period of about three months - the incident described at the beginning of this chapter took place closer to four months from Lauren's hearing those last four words. I realise, in my ability to be rational, that the courts have a job to do, and that they must be thorough, evidence based and as fair as they can be. At the same time, there is something almost cruel about the length of times that things take to happen. They are dealing in objective precision, gathering facts, information, arguing over legal matters. Until I worked with people such as Lauren, I had no real comprehension of the anguish this caused. The tensions not only for Lauren herself, but her children. No wonder her children played up at times, there was a great deal hanging around them. The families are often left to deal with the emotional consequences alone.

Lauren thought she was dealing with the courts to try and protect her children from the influences of a man who had problems with addiction to alcohol, as well as being a known user of drugs. The issue of safety was far worse, as the police officer would reveal to Lauren as they sat down.

THROWN TO THE COURTS

We sat down in the dining room and I looked at the police officer for signs of what she was about to say. My heart was in my mouth, and I could feel the blood pumping in my head.

"I need to tell you that Sophie has made allegations of a sexual nature against Rob, and we need you not to say anything, because we need to get things in order, do things the right way..." she said to me.

I burst into tears. She was telling me what they had to do next - a CP interview, which would take time and it would be a week before they could do anything. I was just beside myself, and I didn't know what to do. I could not take it in. I was feeling really frightened, but what was I frightened of? In some ways it was a relief, a relief that it was finally out. All of this churning worry that I'd carried around with me was released. In other ways it was sheer horror. The horror of it that my very worst nightmares were true. It would have been easier to believe that I was mad. All of this was going around and around, and then it dawned on me.

"Oh my God. Shit. We're back in court tomorrow, what on earth am I going to do?"

LAUREN'S STORY

We were due back in court because of his breaches of the court order and he'd launched a counter-application for unsupervised access, and I didn't know what to do. I just knew he couldn't take my girls. The police are telling me they need a week, and at best I had a day. She was great, the police officer, and promised to go back to the station to file a report, so that it was on the system. She told me I was going to have to get my barrister's advice. That was not so easy as we were due in court at 09:00, and the working day was done. I got there an hour early, just in case they arrived early. My barrister did get there a bit early, with enough time for me to grab her and take her into the ladies toilets and say,

"This is what has happened..." I was terrified.

I didn't want Rob to have any warning about this and I didn't know how they were going to deal with it. The barrister looked at me and said,

"I'm sorry but I am under obligation. I have to inform the court."

"Are you sure?" I replied, "Because the police are worried that he will destroy evidence."

"I am so sorry, but I have to. I am under obligation, because this is now a child protection issue, I am ethically and morally obliged to tell the court right now."

LAUREN'S STORY

We went into the court, and when she announced it, the judge huffed. He huffed. What a great inconvenience to his trial! I could not believe I was hearing him huff. I felt like standing up and chucking something at him. What in the hell are you huffing about? Jesus Christ, I felt like exploding. How dare he huff. He demanded to have the police officer on the phone so that it could be verified. This was the point when my emotions started to cut. It was the point when I thought, 'I am going to be completely on my own on with this...' All the time I was sitting next to Rob, and he was smirking away. I had to stay in this pokey little courtroom with a judge who was huffing, and Rob who was smirking. It was horrendous.

My barrister actually complimented me on my exemplary behaviour. She was so right to. She did not know what I had to sit on and suffer. That evil twisted man and his nightmare solicitor and that huffing judge. This is the madness of the situation. My barrister was acting morally and potentially putting Sophie's case in jeopardy when we should not even have been there. It was his breaches of the order that had forced me back to court in the first place.

I knew Rob would go home and destroy his computer. He did. The police raided him three days later, and found nothing of note on his computers. They did have evidence that his hard drive had been wiped on the afternoon after he'd returned from the family court, but that's not enough to charge someone with child abuse. Sophie had told me that Rob was very keen on photos, and that there were a lot of them. Because her piercings featured in most of them, there would have been no doubt as to who it was. I think that had the police found this evidence, it would not have taken so long to get to trial, and I doubt very sincerely it would have even gone to trial. He would have been advised to plead guilty. As it was, the courts handed him time to get rid of it, and he took it.

Of course, this meant that the courts had to suspend all contact with Rob, which affected the children directly. I was left trying to comfort the kids. It was this totally bizarre situation, like they were so glad that it was out, and that I was protecting them, but at the same time, they would often feel really guilty for getting him into trouble. Their behaviour was extreme. It was like the farce was over and the real shit was coming out now. I was in a complete mess. I coped terribly well on the surface, I am sure most people would have been extremely impressed, but it's not how I felt inside. It was like my soul had been murdered, and I was this robot, just functioning. I felt terribly alone.

I think a lot of people think that you want to kill the person involved - at that point I was less frightened of him. I was more frightened of the authorities, the bigotry, and the sourness. I was more frightened of them, and I had every reason to be.

The police asked me to take Sophie and Jessica down to the interview suite at a hospital nearby. They were going to begin their investigations. Our main contact from the police was Giles. He would be the one to interview the girls, with it being videoed. Jessica was very reluctant to be interviewed, but went in first. When she came out, she was scarlet in the face and very distressed, she ran off into another room and then it was Sophie's turn to be interviewed. I was trying to console Jessica, but she was very agitated about what she had to tell Giles. The police cannot ask questions, because they cannot lead the witness, and so Jessica was very distressed about just having to tell things.

"Just ask me a question..." she would scream at them, because she couldn't find the words through this layer of guilt to tell them what had happened or what she had seen.

LAUREN'S STORY

I attended a conference organised by C'isters in November 2007. One of the workshops was delivered by Robin Watts, who then worked for the Metropolitan Police. The workshop was on how best to respond to disclosures in the criminal justice system. We were in a small group of about 20 people, and most of us were strangers to each other. Robin asked us to sit in pairs, and he would brief us on the exercise. He asked us to describe in full detail what our last sexual encounter had been. The day, time of day, location, description of the room you were in, who initiated it, what exactly had unfolded, what sexual activity you undertook, how long it was for, etc etc. We were all horrified. How could you explain all that to someone you have only just met? He continued with the exercise, long enough to have us all shuffling uncomfortably in our seats. This, however, is not the case for anyone involved in a crime with a sexual nature. These were the kind of facts that Sophie and Jessica had to recount to Giles, a perfect stranger. It is part of the evidence that is needed in a criminal prosecution. This haunts me.

LAUREN'S STORY

Sophie emerged in hysterics. Jessica was also distressed, and still in another room. Sophie ran off into a different room. Which daughter do you go to first? I went back to Jessica, hugged her, and then legged it over to see Sophie. The poor girls were in bits. I couldn't wait to get them home.

I decided that I would take the children away for a few days. We all needed to get away, and I thought the change of scenery would do us all good. The children seemed to calm down a bit. They both wanted to talk to me a bit when they were away, and some of the details came out about how life with Rob had been.

Sophie told me that she loved him, and that they were engaged (with a ring and everything!) and that they were going to get married. She was feeling so guilty for talking to the police. It was incredibly painful listening to her blame herself for everything. The tragic thing about it was that Sophie was in love with him, he had made that happen. She said that she had enjoyed the attention and feeling older. She said that Rob had been blowing in her ear and flirting and that she had enjoyed the attention. She then said that Rob had talked about them having sex but had said a few days later that he said, "I don't think I can go through with this." I thought this was repulsive as it was manipulative, seeming to be rejection and passing

215

blame onto Sophie. I asked her how that had made her feel and she said, "sad." He got her drunk every night and gave her spliffs to smoke. Then one night he got her so drunk she couldn't walk and he had sex with her. This took place in Greece, and it was the point that there was no turning back, Sophie knew that. She'd convinced herself that it wasn't so bad. She focused on the bits that were good, and shut down the fact that she was having sex with her sister's dad. That bit is easy to forget when you're in a 'relationship' and love each other.

I explained to Sophie that all children want attention and that all children flirt sometimes. It is up to adults who know what they are doing to sway the attention the right way. I asked Sophie if she had wanted attention and she said that she could have done without the sex but she enjoyed the attention. I felt really sick and very upset for Sophie. She loved the lavish attention that he gave her, and she felt special. It makes me so sick. I recognise some of the things he did to charm her - he'd done them to me. She felt special, and after that holiday she was in a sexual relationship with him. A deep secret she kept close to herself for a couple of years.

Jessica's stories really disturbed me. She told me of his violence and threats towards her. She said that her dad had lots of knives and that he had bought her a knife. She told me it was so sharp you would cut your finger on it if you only *just* touched it. She said that he had taught her how to use it but had told her that if she didn't use it properly he would use it on her. She truly believed her dad wanted to cut her and hurt her. She said that once her dad had thrown a knife at her and tried to hit her. Jessica told me her daddy had 'cut throats'. I believed her; I remembered his knives. It chilled me to the bone when Sophie later told me that he had bought them both knives. This made me very frightened of him, but I could not show this in front of my children. Both of them were terrified of him.

I am so proud of them, really, I am. They are so resilient.

When we got back from our break, we were back into another round of interviews. Sophie had to have a physical examination and be tested for sexual diseases. Can you imagine what it is like to have to drive your own daughter to be physically examined? It made me sick to the pit of my stomach. It is so awful. I wanted to drive us all far away and never come back but I knew that without the police, we wouldn't be safe from him. We were back into the interview suites again and again. Giles wanted something clarified, or one of the children would remember something, and we had to let them know. Nothing comes out in a straight orderly way. It took the strangest things to trigger a memory, which happens. Sophie would go,

"Oh my God, I'd forgotten that happened."

Like how Rob would break into the house and hide in her wardrobe. At one level it is unbelievable, but this guy is very twisted. The abuse is going back years, remember. I often wonder if the authorities think it seems like embellishment. It was not. It does not come out coherently in a nice neat order and it's all so weird it's hard to take in.

The next thing was that they notified me that they wanted my computer. *My* computer? You're left completely out of control of this situation. The children's behaviour was sometimes vile, bitchy to me, nasty to each other, the house is in complete disarray. The whole thing is this giant mess, and the police walk in and say,

"Right. I'm going to take your computer."

I guessed he'd made some counter-allegation. This interfered directly with my job, so I had to phone my boss and say,

"I'm really sorry, but I don't have my computer. The police have got it."

LAUREN'S STORY

I then had to go in and tell them why. You have to explain to Human Resources what is going on in your private life. I knew my job wasn't going to last much longer. As I said before, I was in a role where I had to be squeaky clean, and I wasn't squeaky anymore.

Rob had been in secret contact with Sophie, seemingly working on her guilt. She had written this note to him which said, "Sorry, I did it for Mum..." I knew why she would say that but it really looked bad to anyone else. This was crucial to their defence. About six months into all of this, Giles contacted me and told me that they were going to give Rob a caution, if he admitted to minor sexual offences. They told me it would be enough to go back to the court with to prevent access, as he'd be placed on a sex offenders register. Great. They had this note from Sophie, which Giles told me would be strong evidence for the defence. It would completely undermine all the evidence that Sophie had provided to them. I could not believe it. The only witness in all of this was Jessica. She had witnessed Rob raping Sophie, but the only person she had told was me. She was very secretive about it, and didn't want me to tell anyone. She said that I could not tell anyone, so I hadn't, up to that point. What a horrendous situation to be in. The case was crumbling in front of me, because of this note from Sophie written in a guilty moment, persuaded by her abuser. The only one who could testify that sex had taken place was my eight-year-old daughter, who had sworn me to secrecy. I had to tell Giles that there was a witness. I said,

"Jessica was awake in the room."

"How do you know that?" he asked,

"Jessica told me."

"Jessica needs to tell us that."

I told him I could not make my daughter tell him that, but at the same time it was unbearable to me that Rob would only get a caution.

"I cannot allow that to happen, but neither can I force my daughter to speak to you."

I was in turmoil, and it took all my courage to speak to Jessica later that evening. I told her that what she had told me, I had to tell Giles, because Daddy was not going to face charges for hurting Sophie. I told her that Giles needed to hear it from her. It was an awful, heartbreaking situation. I didn't want her going back into that interview room, having seen what it had done to her before. If she'd turned round to me and said, "I am not going to do it," my heart would have broken again, but I would have accepted it. But she said with confidence,

"I will do it."

LAUREN'S STORY

She did. It was so distressing. We had to go back into the interview suite so that she could be interviewed and videoed again. She was running in and out of the room, begging them again to ask her questions. But they could not. She told them that Rob had sex with Sophie, but then she had to prove she knew what sex was. She had to show them with dolls and things like that. This is because people have got off in the past because direct questions apparently put suggestions into the child's mind. There has to be no room for doubt in the eyes of the law. It is disgusting. It is evil what you have to go through because of the evil of these people.

Lauren and her children were put through a horrendous ordeal in order to try and ensure a criminal prosecution for the offences against Sophie. Unfortunately, the trauma that is experienced by the family in going through the legal process of the courts is not unique. We already have Kelly's perspective of it, and now we have Lauren's. It is a very difficult line to tread. I believe that every police officer involved in the prosecution of child sex offenders wants to see the perpetrators locked up - secure in prison it means that one less paedophile is abusing children. The police have a tough job, because they have to deal with the objectivity of an evidence-based legal system. However, the action of giving evidence can re-traumatise the child in reliving the experiences, and lead to prolonged emotional and behavioural problems. I can really understand why Lauren was in turmoil, because the abuse was alive and among them. I am not sure of where I stand. Of course I want those who have committed these horrendous crimes against children dealt with, and children protected, but the costs to the family of going through the court process are very high.

As if Lauren did not have enough to deal with, her work situation changed, and she was rejected by another body in her life.

My job - this was just about the last straw and in some ways not that surprising. Just at the time when all of this was going on, I got made redundant. My job was suddenly 'surplus to requirements'. What, despite the fact that I'd won them countless awards over ten years? The fact that I had earned them millions over the years, literally millions? Suddenly I was no longer required. Every cloud has its silver lining, and although I was totally gutted, I thought 'great, this gives me a chance to be a full-time mum.' Only the children didn't want me either. I felt so tainted. Just disgusting. I was full of so much self-loathing. I felt that everyone was out to persecute me, yet none of this was my fault. I had been brutalised by CAFCASS and the family court, the police were very sceptical of me, I had been ostracised at work, a lot of my friends had, well, disappeared saying they "couldn't cope with it... " It was the most horrible, horrible time. And we had to just wait and wait.

It took two years to get to court. Two years!

During those two years we were so alone. The professionals deal with you in terms of the evidence that you bring, not the aching, breaking human beings that we all were. For two years the children were not able to get any therapy. Therapists have to treat all sessions before the trial as potential evidence, they have to record sessions or have two people in the room. The therapists are likely to get called to court. We were turned down by a number of organisations because they didn't have the resources for all of this. The general view of the criminal courts is that therapists apparently put ideas in children's minds, which can undermine the evidence. Although this is not the official line, therapy before the trial is not encouraged. You also have to remember that your children's therapy notes can get called into the courts. The defence get to see everything, all statements, videos, notes, everything. They had two years to review all of this and build up their arguments, when we're living in this kind of hell. The children were having nightmares, night terrors, because they had spoken out against Rob. They were so frightened about this. Sophie woke from her sleep screaming and sweating, and Jessica wet the bed, most nights more than once.

How do you cope with this?

I was lucky, I found Mosac. I was so alone, so desperate. I felt that my life was over. I was offered a short set of counselling appointments and this woman suggested I contacted Mosac. It was there I found the kindness and professionalism that the children and I needed. At Mosac, they nodded knowingly when I tried to describe and make sense of all the lies and manipulation. It was at Mosac that the behaviour of my children was understood. I met other mothers and realised that I wasn't alone and that my story was frighteningly similar to theirs. It was when I met the other, lovely, capable ladies there that I realised I wasn't an idiot or a bad mother. What a gift. Mosac gave me back enough sanity and strength to nurse my children, nurse myself and get through the court case. They were the only people I felt completely safe with and who came to court for the trial to support us. I would find out just how much we would need to lean on them during the case.

The day it came to court, our barrister was delayed on another case, and so we were allocated a new one. The day of the trial. They have two years, and we get a guy showing up on the day. It was one horror after the next. I am furious about this, and no one says anything. A jury should know things like this. As if waiting two years wasn't bad enough, each day we'd come to court and they would keep delaying the case. "Come back tomorrow." Day after day. It was torture on all of us.

When it finally began properly, on day one they watched the video, which Sophie also had to watch sitting in the witness box, and then afterwards there are interviews. Only, because of all the delays, it was Friday when they got to the video, and Sophie was told to come back after the weekend to face questions. How cruel is that? Your daughter's words, tears, hurt are viewed publicly by all, and she has to wait until after the weekend to have the rest of it done with. Why doesn't the judge stop that from happening? It seems so immoral to me. It's so offensive to me, I was so mad. Can you imagine how hurt she was over that weekend? She was in an absolute mess, it had completely re-traumatised her. She was terrified of saying the wrong thing, not remembering things exactly, of getting tripped up by the defence. I kept on saying to her that she went through it, so she will remember when prompted, but it was so hard for her.

Sophie was completely shattered by Monday. We went into court, and she spent two days on the witness stand. It's disgusting. I was not allowed in court, as I was also a witness. I was not allowed to know about the case, and therefore not allowed to support her. I had to sit and wait outside. Thank God for Mosac, they stayed in court with her.

When it was my time to go on the stand, I was so nervous. It didn't help matters seeing Rob there. I was really frightened and repulsed by it. There was a police officer standing in front of him, so that in theory the police officer blocked him for me, but Rob sort of lay out along the dock to see around the police officer. He just sneered at me. It was awful. Why don't they stop this kind of thing? Why don't they stop this antagonistic behaviour? Does anyone in the court even notice? He smirked at me as the defence made me out to be a complete cow, blocking access and stuff like that. My barrister did nothing at all, because he did not know the case. The defence also produced a sworn affidavit from CAFCASS saying that I was trying to interfere with access, and that I was prepared to use my children to do that. I was absolutely gob-smacked. Stunned. I didn't know what to make of it. And still my barrister did nothing. I thought that this was it now; the case had turned from being about Sophie, into this farce.

They had also called the parents of Sophie's friends into the court as witnesses, so they were on the stand. I had to tolerate their anger towards me, like I was to blame. I did not know Rob was in contact with their daughters, taking them places. I was not living with him, had nothing to do with him as a person. I had no idea, but I had to tolerate their shouting and fury. How was I supposed to know what was happening? Did they think for one minute that if I'd known I would have said,

"Well that's fine..."

Every one just wants to heap blame on you.

Then they decided they wanted Sophie to face more questioning, so they hauled her back in. Wasn't it enough trauma? I could not believe it.

After two weeks of the trial the jury were dismissed to make their decision. Oh My Goodness. This was about the worst part of the whole court experience for me. Decision time. My bones felt like they were on fire, right to the inside of my bones, from all this stress and fear. Giles, the police officer, was really good, trying to reassure me. He was telling me all of these stories, and I did appreciate it. I have no idea how I survived that waiting. The jury took $4^{1/2}$ hours to come back with a decision. I could not cope with going back into the court, so Giles went in with Mosac, but I didn't want to see Rob again. I couldn't bear it. I was shaking all over. I was pacing up and down. The lady from Mosac then came bursting into the room, crying, and I thought, 'oh God, he's got off.' She was shaking, but she saw the panic registering on my face, and was saying,

"No, no, no - he's guilty."

I just burst into tears. Great tears rolled down my face. Both of us were sobbing, howling, like wounded animals. I cannot believe what we went through.

As Lauren recalled this part of her story, she broke down. Her body shook as sounds convulsed from her - an echo of the sobs she released that day still evident in her still. She told me that, at the time, their noise was so disturbing that someone from Witness Support rushed in to see what was happening. This does not surprise me in the slightest, because of what is buried deep within her. I also am not certain it is anything that will ever leave her, so deep is the

LAUREN'S STORY

wound caused by actions of the man that hurt and abused her children. This guilty man. The relief of the decision created an immediate release of tension. The sense of being heard, understood and validated must have been a very powerful feeling. The twelve men and women of the jury had witnessed the plight of her and her daughters, judging in a way that the professional services had not. For the first time since the police officer dealt with the assault claims, Lauren felt heard.

Unlike Donald in Kelly's story, Rob was held in custody. There would be no four weeks for him to get his life in order. Sentencing was held over for six weeks, but when Lauren left court, she knew that Rob would remain in prison. It provided a degree of protection that she had been longing for, for a very long time. The sentence that was awarded was for five years. If he behaves himself in prison he could be reduced in $2^{1/2}$ years. That's a little over the time it took to come to court. The sentence is derisory, but in terms of the law, and what is within guidance, it was good news.

Lauren left the court with a sense of freedom that she had not felt for many years. Freedom from Rob, knowing that he was secure behind bars, and free from the judgements that had hounded her. Lauren examines the

LAUREN'S STORY

impact of the court process on her, and reflects on her experiences.

OUR LIFE IS GIVEN BACK TO US BUT WHAT REMAINS?

I remember going home, feeling so sleepy and tired. I lay on the bed with Jessica and Sophie, and I was stroking their hair saying,

"It's OK, it's over, it's OK..."

Jessica was initially so relieved that he had been locked away where he was no threat to her or Sophie. We all snuggled up together and fell asleep. I was in a deep sleep for the first time in two years. However, I woke up at 6:00 the next morning in such incredible pain.

I'd gone to sleep so relieved and so exhausted - like I'd just run around the earth to save my children - and I woke in the most awful pain in my back and legs. I woke moaning. I felt I could not move, the pain was so awful, but I had to try and stop this pain. I was hunting in the bathroom for some painkillers, and then I started vomiting. Dry vomit, retching uncontrollably. I have been in pain ever since that day - I can't even say if the pain was there before but that the adrenaline constantly pumping through me had kept it at bay, but since then, I have been in pain. It is getting easier, not so bad since I am getting stronger. I get the nausea too, when I'm thinking about what happened. It comes out of nowhere, but as I am building myself back up, it comes less.

It took me a month before I could do anything, get outside even. I was just too exhausted and wounded. The relief that came so quickly left us so quickly too. What we are left with is a legacy of hurt and pain.

The trouble with euphoria is that it is short-lived. It is an intense and extremely heightened sensation, but it does not last. Does it make up for all of the anguish Lauren had experienced over the years? The picture of serenity that Lauren paints on that first night with Jessica and Sophie perhaps suggests it does, and I understand that sense of peace and stillness. How welcome that must have been. Lauren is able to let go for the first time in over two years. The gift of sleep on that one night was precious. I wish that it had lasted longer for Lauren, and it disturbs me that her body seems to have broken when the good news has sunk in. Energetically her body must have had just about had all that it could take, after all, running round the earth is an exhausting feat. So, after the euphoria passed, there was nothing, as Lauren, Sophie and Jessica tried to return to a new sense of normality.

LAUREN'S STORY

In finding their new normality, Lauren also had to mend her tired body, rebuild her inner strength and learn to heal. Part of that process was on reflecting on what had passed, turning it over, making it fit, and learning to accept it. I had asked Lauren some specific questions about her experience, looking back. The first was where she saw the low points as being.

The low points? My God there were so many.

Dealing with the authorities was frustrating and soul-destroying. They had so much power over us, and we were so lost because of some of the things that they did. Decisions were made that I just could not fathom. I wasn't allowed to know any details about what had happened. I only knew what my children chose to tell me so I was often confused by their behaviour. How is a parent supposed to help their child if they don't know what's happened to them? Why do they separate the child off when they interview them? I understand the logic of it, but it makes secrets between themselves and the child, my child. It is just like Rob did with them - they are replicating the behaviour of the abuser; Jessica was very confused by this.

LAUREN'S STORY

What could she tell me if I wasn't being told by the police? What did she have to preserve? What might have been the implied threats - not from the authorities directly, but fears established by Rob? She was in a complete mess after being interviewed. There must be ways that this situation can be improved, without compromising objectivity and evidence. I wish I had been shown respect regarding the knowledge I have about my children. I didn't feel that the authorities were working with me, or wanting to work with me, at all. I felt excluded and patronised. I really had no power, they had it all. Giles, the police officer, was very good with us and we grew to like him as time passed, but at the end of the day he's there to do a job.

Giles after the case was heard, told me that he was worried about me in the court. He said that I was the one who he was most worried about giving evidence and screwing it all up. I could not believe it. It's so undermining. What on earth did he think I would do?

"You were in such a state," he said.

Of course I fucking was. What an understatement. Don't they get how much it rips you apart?

You think that when a child finally tells what's been going on that everything will be fine from that point and you can nurse them better but that's not how it worked for us. The thing that stopped the healing process and horrified me was finding out how much my children despised me. This is all thanks to Rob's lies, the stories he concocted over the time the children were with him. I know now that all abusers will use separation techniques to isolate the child from the person they are closest to. All that time when access was going well, when I had no idea, he was poisoning their minds, drip-feeding them obscenities about me, their mother. He'd shown them filthy pornographic pictures, really dirty sexual pictures, and said to them,

"That's what your mum does when she's got rid of you to me..."

He told them I wanted to abort them both, that I had £70,000 in savings and that he was paying for their upkeep. He said I was a greedy bitch, working only for money, and that as soon as they were 16, I was going to chuck them out. He fed them this stream of constant hatred, all the time brewing this deep resentment, over years. I had to try not to feel aggrieved that they would so easily believe him but it was really hard sometimes.

Of course finding out the truth initially was horrendous. That initial trauma when you just go to jelly and you literally fall apart. I felt like the life was being sucked from my soul. After I picked myself up from that, to be strong for them, the lasting trauma for me has been finding out that that they hated me so much. I wanted to believe that if I loved them enough, I could take their pain away. I could help them heal. I had been so lied about, that it made it very difficult. As children, they wanted to be rescued from him and this terrible situation. They expected me to rescue them, but I knew nothing. I understand their need. In their minds, I had failed them twice - because of the vile things they believed about me, and because I did not know about it to be able to rescue them. I was their mother after all, I knew everything didn't I?

As much as I love my children, some of my lowest points have been when I've thought 'what's the point in my being here? You hate my guts and sometimes I feel like it's too much for me to look after you when you hate me. I am trying to give my soul to you, and you just don't want it...' The exhaustion of your children needing you so much but making it hard for you to get close to them creates resentment in your head. And then the sensible, loving mummy comes out and you go, 'don't be so bloody dramatic, things will get better...' And then you remember what they've been through, and it kind of shunts you back. But when you are being attacked by the people you are trying to heal, and you have given up everything to do that.

Everything. And they don't want it. It felt like everything
- my heart, my body, and my life – I poured into my family
had been ripped away from me in such a deep and dark
way. I'm not talking about the normal rebellion of a, "I
hate you Mum," kind of child, but this dark, venomous hurt
that comes from your abused, confused and angry children.
The revulsion they had towards me at times. I felt
weakened by it, and often held to ransom, because you
want them to understand that you love them. But at times
I felt like screaming at them,

"How dare you! Shut up! Don't you dare speak to
me like that!"

You want to put some boundaries back, and they are
pushing against them. Sometimes I did end up shouting,
and then the immediate remorse I felt. 'Oh my God. I just
shouted at my children. Screamed at them...' This endless
cycle of hatred and hurt. They didn't want me to touch
them, because I repulsed them so much, but at other times
they were so demanding of me as a 'mummy'. It's like I was
constantly being pulled and pushed - "nurse me, clean up
after me, help me" - and then, "get away from me..." I was
clearing up the mess that was left behind. For Jessica, it
was literally cleaning up her bed three times a night after
she had wet, and Sophie was staying out late and coming
home angry, emotional, and upset so that I would end up

half the night trying to soothe her. This nightly mopping up and nursing, only for their hatred to return the next morning, so this whole process began again. You feel so fucking alone. That was another thing. Everyone around you is patronising, rude, or can't handle the situation. Many people disappeared from my life, some have tried to come back, once the verdict was known, but I don't want to deal with that kind of friendship, support. Mosac was the only consistent point of sanity I had throughout all of this and I owe them so much. Having that understanding of what no one else seems to be able to deal with.

These days it is less that I feel the persecution from them, it's less prevalent, but it's still there.

I am curious as to why she experiences the persecution as less these days. What has changed, in her or her children, that it feels less potent?

I suppose now, that frantic awful desperate state I existed in for the time leading up to the trial, the two years of terror we suffered, meant that everything was tense and heightened. You are living and reacting off your nerves in a very uncentred way. The terror has subsided, and so I am not so controlled by it. I have a good sense of myself again, and I am more at ease with myself. I've done a lot of work on myself, and therefore the potency of the venom from my children have has worn off. They stopped getting a reaction from me, and therefore they slowly stopped pushing as it was not having the same effect. They have relaxed in my company, and are seeing the real mummy, the strong, kind mummy more these days. His lies have been absent and their potency has worn off. It is much better.

We worked with a psychologist for a while, and she told me that I was living in the past. I can't get out of the past. It is with us. Every time I think we're going forward, something else comes out, and we are pulled back. I am dealing with the effects of the past, and it's here now in our lives. Don't tell me I'm living in the past, because that's just not true. It is here and now, and we are trying to deal with it. It is very hard at times, and so draining, but when you know and understand something, accept the hideousness, then you have a point from which you can move on. At least, that's how it is for me.

It does still go on, and the effects of his abusing them can crop up every day. You have to be ready for it. It can be a daily battle, which I am at times never sure I will ever win. But you do battle on. I have read some good books in the process of trying to put myself back in one piece, and I have calmed down a great deal.

I have sworn a great deal. For some time I swore at God every day. I didn't lose my faith, but I called God a lot of names. Of all the nasty things that could have happened in my life, hurting my children was the very worst thing, so I was really angry with God. I eventually stopped swearing at Him, and after then I found a new peace, a different peace. This has been one very good thing to happen - it wasn't there before. This internal peace. A peace that notices that even in the worst of times with my children, we laughed together. A peace that knows that even when there is so much evil put into your life, there is some goodness. You cannot keep the goodness down. Somewhere in the midst of all of this stuff, there is still compassion, still love, still something to be salvaged.

Lauren's faith has been important to her, and it seems that there is a parallel in forgiving her God and finding her inner strength, and peace. At the same time, I know that this has not been accompanied by a sense of justice, and yet the two somehow co-exist for me. I have a sense of injustice

LAUREN'S STORY

from knowing Lauren's story, but it is important for me that she is able to articulate for herself, so I ask her if she believes that justice has been served.

No, justice has not been served. The man is dangerous because he comes across as so not dangerous. He has committed a lot of crimes in his life, and yet those were always overlooked as being 'not that bad'. He had drugs convictions - possession of Class A drugs and possession of Class B drugs with intent to supply. He had firearms cautions. He was once held on remand for a plot to kidnap someone very senior in our country. He had all those knives. But don't worry, he's 'not that bad'. What? I found out these convictions in criminal court. How dangerous he actually was came out in court. How is that missed in the family court, why is it not brought in? How can excluding that have possibly been right for the safety of the children? No, justice has not been served. I feel quite frightened for when he comes out from his sentence, this half sentence, because I believe he will seek revenge. He frightens me.

There are injustices which we experienced that I feel are not being dealt with. I have complained, officially, and they are not being dealt with. I am still getting the brush off. Will justice be served over my treatment in family court? I doubt it. There is so much secrecy, and I fear it will not be worth getting into trouble over. However, I do have a moral sense of duty to protect other children, children in situations that I don't know about. I have been to my MP, humiliated myself with this story, and he has written to the government Minister for Children, Young People and Families, but we simply got brushed off, we haven't had a reply. No one is interested.

The thing that troubles me the most is that Rob still has full parental responsibility over Jessica. If I die tomorrow, he is the one, by law, who will take charge of my estate. I can't move without his permission or take the children abroad for more than a few weeks without his consent. Parental responsibility cannot be removed; well it can, but only by the court. It is not automatically removed when there is a conviction for crimes against children. Who is going to go to court if I am not here? It is an unbelievable flaw in the law. He is a convicted child sex offender, he will be on the sex offenders register, and yet he still has control over us, over his very victims. Everyone assumes that the courts protect you and deal with it, but who is going to pay to have that acted on? I've been told it will cost £20,000 - £30,000 to have his parental responsibility removed. Where am I supposed to get that kind of money from? Legal aid will just get put as a debt on my home. According to the letters I have received from the Department for Children, removing parental responsibility from this monster is a matter the courts have to deliberate very seriously. What? There should be nothing to deliberate. I should be able to put a letter into the court, now, for it to be stamped. Bang. Your rights as a parent are revoked because you sexually abuse children. But no. We have to protect the rights of parents, fathers. Where is the welfare of the child in all of this?

It sounds like an unbelievable story, doesn't it? People won't believe what I went through and what rights he still has. I sometimes don't believe it. I still feel sick to the pit of my stomach how close it came to the children being handed over to him by the family court. I have never done anything wrong in all of this; I was only ever trying to protect my children. There was so much evidence, even before the criminal trial, how unsuitable he was for unsupervised access, let alone custody. And yet even after his conviction for abusing them, he still he has protection as Jessica's father. I can't rest until this injustice in family law is resolved.

This is why single mums, vulnerable women, are being targeted by paedophiles.

LAUREN'S STORY

If I were to offer any advice from these experiences, I would say to trust your instincts. Women are often less confident about their feelings, we are often told we are too emotional or made to feel stupid about 'having a feeling'. Our instincts are powerful, as I know now, and shouldn't be ignored. That feeling about him in the beginning, when I first knew him, that I couldn't explain, turned out to be spot on. I wish that I had acted upon this with stronger conviction, and then none of the horrors that have happened would have taken place, because I'd have said,

"You know, there is no Rob and Lauren. Goodbye."

This is to you reading this, if this is resonating somewhere. If you feel that there is something not quite right or that you are being lied to, manipulated or treated unfairly, you are probably right. You don't owe an explanation to anyone, trust in yourself and explore your feelings thoroughly. If you feel you are being trivial, or like me, there is no evidence to back up how you feel, please remember that you may never know everything or have proof. Please remember that as a decent person, you may not be able to imagine the horrors someone else can invoke on you and your family. You are worth protecting so trust your feelings.

LAUREN'S STORY

Parental responsibility is a dreadful trap for Lauren and Jessica to still be under. In wanting to write with as much accuracy as I could, I checked it out. It is correct, as it stands in law now. It is a deeply troubling fact that Jessica could be handed over to Rob in the event of Lauren's death, because he has parental responsibility. Parental responsibility in her case was assigned by the courts, but now, post 1 December 2003, it is the name of the father on the child's birth certificate (except in cases of adoption, of course). For the single mums reading this, take care. Once on, it cannot easily be removed. It seems, to me at least, that the law makers have lost all sense in not tightening up on this provision. Do we really want convicted child sex offenders holding onto the rights of parental responsibility?

This really does haunt Lauren. She wants to do more to raise awareness of the risks to our children if this remains the case. Preventing child abuse is hard enough, but when weaknesses in the law permeate strategies for child sex offenders, then I agree with her. More has to be done. It is hard to make any one listen.

Finally, Lauren reflects on how she sees herself in the awful situation she found herself in. She marvels at herself, and rightly so. Lauren is an exceptional woman, incredibly brave, and her children are truly blessed that she never gave up the fight for them.

I look back and see all the places that people tried to blame me for what happened, but they don't need to do this, because no one blames themselves more than I do. It's like looking back at pieces of it, and fitting it together. Rob was the one with the script, no one else, and he knew where he was steering everyone, me, the kids, family, friends and the authorities. He duped everyone. I was just a pawn, and it didn't matter how I reacted to something, because he had the strings. My reactions, even if he hadn't foreseen them, would have been used against me. I am trying to forgive myself for how I was in this game, and the reality of how I coped with a sex offender.

I have responded, and I have kept fighting. I am so proud of myself for this. I have always stood my ground, in the face of him, his parents, the police, the family courts, because I have been resolute in the protection of my children. I learned early on that I was, and am, the most important cog in the wheel. It's true that as soon as you start to repair yourself, mend your shattered self-esteem, then everything else starts to follow, not immediately, but it does follow. I had to hang on to myself to fight for them. And when the trial was over, I was still fighting for them. It has been a different battle, where you're fighting your own demons and those of your children, but it is worth the fight. I am worth the fight. My children are worth the fight.

JANE & MATT'S
STORY

JANE & MATT'S STORY

Jane and Matt live on the edge of a sleepy village in southern England. They are a professional couple, with successful careers in creative industries. They run their own business, having launched it earlier this year. Their house is charming, an old farm cottage surrounded by fields. They have two children - Gavin, now aged eleven, and Philippa who is now eight. Both attend the local primary school in the village, and family life revolves around the children, with various after school activities and sporting fixtures. There is a lot of love in this household.

Jane and Matt make a handsome couple. I sense there is a deep and tender connection between them, evident even when they are telling a story of difference and conflict. They are caring people, for each other, for their children, but also for their society. They are community minded, both supporting local activities in their village. They come from close families, and are proud of where they have ended up. They are both intelligent, thinkers. They work hard, striving to provide opportunities for their children. Despite all of this, they did not see what was happening within their own family, their support systems. Never let it be said that childhood sexual abuse is limited to a benefit class of low achievement and low intelligence.

They are both open with me, giving their stories freely despite the pain it clearly gives in reliving some of the details. They want it told so that other people can benefit and know that there is no need to feel alone. They are champions of Mosac, and are still left with a deep sense of injustice from 'the system.'

THE NIGHT OUR LIFE
CHANGED

I meet Jane and Matt as a couple for the interviews, but as we are going over the background to this project, they surprise me saying that they want their stories told separately. They want their own voices to be heard, because, they tell me, their experiences are so different. Trusting them as experts in their experiences, I of course agree. I could not have imagined how different their stories and how valuable their contributions would be.

Jane is a caring host. She checks that I have everything I need and that I am comfortable. She speaks about the effort of my journey to see them, startling me, as I am the stranger that has appeared in the midst of a summer evening, with a recording device to take from them their stories. It is they, surely, who are about to make all the effort. Jane has a high degree of empathy, which becomes more evident to me as her story unfolds. It is this empathy that at times seems to wrap itself around her, as she worries about the feelings of everyone close to her. This has slowed her ability to process over the last couple of years, as she tries to navigate through what is best to do. I know that Jane is an artist, but I am also struck by a degree of organisation and order in her process, which I had not expected. Possibly my stereotype of an artist, but the structure in the way she presents things impresses me. She has to think things through, carefully, and has a steely determination to get through the situation presented to her.

Matt has the appearance of a regular guy who works out, and looks after himself. The emotional strain that he speaks of is not visible, so he hides his fragility well. I learn that he holds onto his feelings, and is gracious allowing Jane to work through things at her own pace. Matt's process is lightning quick, and as a consequence sits longer than Jane with resolved feelings and thoughts. He has taken a massive amount of emotional strain, and yet you just would not know this if you were to meet him for the first time. There is an intensity about him, a passion. My guess is that this is what fires him up on the sports field, but this force has a darker edge for him too. He cares deeply for Jane and his children, and at the same time is crippled by the belief that he has failed in his role as a father, a protector.

JANE & MATT'S STORY

Jane and Matt have been married for fourteen years. They have faced some difficulties, as all couples do, but nothing has tested their bond like this ordeal. In 2007, they accidentally found out that their daughter was being sexually abused. It was Jane that made the discovery, and therefore their story starts with her.

I was the one who found out about this situation, with our daughter, Philippa. It took place in this room. I was in here with the children, just lazing around. Philippa and Gavin were playing on the sofa and I was sitting on the armchair over by the fireplace. Gavin was reclined on the sofa, and Philippa was sitting on top of him, moving around and jigging up and down a bit. She said those words that just made my heart sink, she said,

"When I sit on Granddad's knee, a bit like this, he gets his willy out..."

I remember thinking to myself that there just couldn't be any other explanation for that. I jumped into this 'don't-know-what-to-do-but-must-do-something-but-don't-overreact-mummy.' I sat there, quite calmly, and I didn't say a word. Inside I was churning away; this turmoil that began from nowhere. I remember this hideous sinking

255

feeling in my stomach, and at the same time I knew I couldn't go where it was taking me. It's hard to describe, but this mother-instinct just kicked in. I knew I had to be strong for my children from this moment onwards.

Philippa then said that she wanted to go to the toilet, so I said I'd take her, thinking that it was my chance to check out what I'd heard. If Gavin had heard something, he didn't react to her, so I knew it was up to me to check what she'd said.

Philippa was sitting on the toilet, and I was perched on the bath. I asked her about what she'd said. I wanted to be gentle, so that she wasn't alarmed, but I really needed to confirm it.

"What did you mean about Granddad, Philippa?" I asked in this really soft voice. She just reiterated what she'd said before, and I didn't want to react, so I think I said something like, "oh, that's odd..." and she went back to her game. We had to take Gavin to his sports club, and Philippa and I always sit at the back watching and waiting for him. I'm sitting there wondering what to say, with all these thoughts tramping through my head. I thought I'd gently probe some more, desperate not to just fire off all these questions at her. I didn't want to make her worried or upset, but at the same time, I knew I had to try to elicit some facts to move it forward. I said to her,

JANE & MATT'S STORY

"You know you told me that about that thing with Granddad, well, where does it happen?"

"At their house, Mummy," she replied.

At Granddad and Grandma's house! They had an attic room, like an office. I then asked her how many times it had happened, so I raised my hands indicating 'five' or 'many' (flashing lots of hands). She was still of an age if I'd have said 20 or 100, she wouldn't have known, but she said like the first hand. I could gauge a few times, at least. Of course, this is only one side of the story, but in all likelihood it is the most truthful and accurate.

When we came back from the sports club, it was time for the children to go to bed. Philippa didn't seem to be worried about it, or anxious or anything. She was like her normal self going to bed, but she asked me,

"Mummy, is it going to happen again?"

"No, darling, it wasn't the right thing for Granddad to do."

God, I didn't know what to say to her. I was so unprepared for what to say to her. It was very wrong what he did to her, and yet I didn't want to scare her. I also told her that if she ever wanted to talk to me about anything to do with that, then she could. Anything, worries, anything.

"You must feel you can talk to Mummy."

I also said that it was probably best she talked to me about it, and not other people. It was so tricky, you don't want to make it a big taboo, but you also want to protect her from other people's reactions. I didn't know how to deal with it. Nothing prepares you for this situation. It was so important to me that she could talk about it, but I wanted to be her safe haven at that point. I couldn't say Daddy at that point, because he didn't know. It was a very odd situation. Still, she went off to sleep just like any other night, leaving me alone with a million thoughts rampaging through my head.

I didn't know what to do next. What do you do? Do I tell Matt? I knew I had to tell him, but when should I tell him? I had all of these feelings about my father going through my head. It was awful, and I didn't sleep a wink that night. During the night, what I decided to do was to tell my sister, Clara, because I thought I could just relay it to her and get some kind of opinion. She was Philippa's aunty, my sister and moreover another dynamic in the family situation. I had to tell her, it suddenly felt really clear. Not a friend, not Matt, not my mother. It was my only instinct at the time, and I had to listen to it.

It was the worst of timing, because the following day my mum and I were going up to London to spend a day with Clara. My father was due to be collecting the children from school, and taking them back to their place. I knew that couldn't happen, but I couldn't tell my mum. I couldn't let on that something was wrong until I'd seen my sister, so I had to create an excuse when my parents came to the house the following day.

The next morning, I dropped the children off at school and came back to speak to my sister. I had to tell her before I saw her so that we could keep Mum out of the picture. I was literally shaking as I picked up the phone.

"I've got something to tell you, and I'm really scared and so worried," I began,

"Philippa imparted some information last night, and I don't know what to do, and I've got to tell Matt..."

"I'll stop you there," she said, "it's Dad, isn't it?"

And of course I knew from that what the next thing was going to be.

"Oh God! It didn't happen to you, did it?"

"Yes, it did..."

Clara was 43 at the time and had been living with the secret of her own abuse for 30 years. I had no idea absolutely no idea. She immediately got upset, saying,

"If ever I thought something like that was going to happen, I thought it would be later on, and I was getting myself ready to tell you, to warn you..."

She had all these feelings of guilt, even though she had no need to. She had told one friend at the time. It never amounted to full sexual intercourse, but it was bad enough.

I gathered every ounce of strength I had as I waited for my parents to arrive, so that Mum and I would continue up to London. When they walked in, I said to Dad,

"Look, I'd prefer it today if Gavin stayed at school and did this other sports activity he wants to try, and I need to get back, so we'll see you at the school...."

"Oh, don't worry yourself, it's fine, you come to me later...."

And of course, all these hideous thoughts are going through my head about my father, and my stomach is in free fall.

"That's what is going to happen because I need to get back," made the end of it. I said some really lame excuse, and that was that. I knew what I had to aim at to keep my children safe; keep them out of my parents' home.

Going to London with Mum was so hard, and my sister had engineered it so that we had some time together. She'd arranged for Mum to have a beauty treatment. I walked around London in a daze that day. Mum clearly had no idea about any of it. I knew that the next stage was going to be telling Matt, but I had no idea how I was going

JANE & MATT'S STORY

to do that. I didn't know what to think myself, let alone try
to make sense of it to him. I had no idea how he would
react, other than, as her father, be totally devastated. I
didn't know if he'd pick up his keys and go round and try to
kill my father. I wanted my sister to be there too, so we
agreed that she and her husband would come over for the
evening, and that I'd tell him when they were both there. I
don't know why I wanted it this way, but it just felt right to
have Clara there too.

We came back from London early, as I had planned,
and Mum and I went to the school to get the children.
Gavin was out on the field and Philippa was inside, so I
said to Mum that she should wait for Philippa, and that I'd
walk up with Dad to collect Gavin. Something had turned
inside me, and as we walked, I just could not hold it in
anymore. I had to say something to him, I wanted him to
know I knew about his sordid behaviour. I walked with
him up this little road, and turned to him.

"I know what you've done to Philippa. I know what
you did to Clara. It is going to stop. If you come within an
inch of my daughter, I will put a restraining order on you..."

"Oh, I'm really sorry. It is going to stop. It has
stopped. I don't know what happened."

He was this pathetic, crushed little man and it was
just like talking to a stranger. Every bit of my history, as a

family, seemed to be wiped out. Gone. It was really odd. I don't know, it was just really weird.

As Jane is recalling this part of the story her voice falters, and she catches herself as she begins to cry. Matt places a hand on her arm, squeezing it gently. I can see that Jane wants to regain her composure quickly, but I am struck by the seemingly sudden surge of pain. I ask her if this pain gets any less.

"Not really," she replies, "it sort of goes on the back burner, and I haven't talked like this about it for ages, so it flares up, and it's there. Suddenly it's there again."

The situation that Jane is facing is horrific, and I marvel at the calmness that she exuded at the time. She seems determined not to flap, and make a terrible situation much worse. There seems to be a solidity in her. Her losses are huge within a 24 hour period; she has discovered her daughter has been sexually abused, her sister was also sexually abused by the man she has called "Dad" all her life. Her own history has been vapourised, and it impresses me that she retains this groundedness, when everything she knew as solid and safe has been shaken. I suspect her own pain was buried then, as she struggled to move from one stage to the next. Next was to tell Matt, which was a mounting source of guilt and betrayal inside her. This is where Matt joins the story, and we move between them as events unfold.

OUR WORLD COLLAPSES

Jane: It was another night before I told Matt. I was all churned up from talking to my father, and I'd arranged with Clara that she and Nick, her husband, would come over the following night. I could not have kept it from Matt for much longer. I felt that I was betraying him for not telling him, so, it was just awful. All these hideous emotions inside of me. Clara hadn't been able to tell Nick at all. When they came over that following night, she'd ended up telling him about herself as they were walking up to the front door. I felt so sorry for him. She had to tell him, because those kind of questions were going to be asked among the four of us, "did it happen to you?"

We all sat down in the living room, and Matt had no idea what was coming towards him. I'd just told him that they were coming over for the evening, and they'd be there when Matt got back from work.

Matt: I had no idea what had gone on for Jane in the days leading up to this evening. I just came home from work one day and Jane's sister and her husband were here, which I found a bit strange as we'd never been that close before. I assumed it was just a social visit, and it wasn't until the kids were in bed, and Jane had made a drink. She came in here and sat down. She came straight out with it, and said,

"I've got something terrible to tell you..."

It was a millisecond and I thought that she was going to say that she had cancer, or there was something terribly wrong with one of the kids. In that fraction of a second, I had a whole support network worked out in my head, literally, all worked out in my head, 'we'll get through this, no big deal,' I was thinking and then BANG. She told me that her dad had abused Philippa. It was just an unbelievable shock. I just.... how are you supposed to cope with that? I'm not prepared for that. I don't know how we should deal with that...

The first thing I said was,

"Did it happen to either of you two?"

Jane didn't say a word, but I looked across at her sister, who was welling up, and I just knew she'd been abused too. She didn't say anything then, but she didn't have to.

At first I felt disbelief, I didn't believe that he would have done something like that, then it sort of shifted a bit, for some Godforsaken reason, some misplaced sympathy for him. Why on earth would he do something like that? I thought that he must be in some really dark place to have stooped so low as to have done something like that.

JANE & MATT'S STORY

Our initial conversations about him that evening were trying to work out how we could help him, but even towards the end of that first evening of knowing, I was slipping down the lines of,

"We have got to go to the police about this...."

That's where I remained, in this position, which wasn't what Jane or Clara wanted to do. I felt very differently about it.

Jane: Matt's first reaction of pity towards my father was not what I was expecting at all. This kind of "what a pathetic, sick man to do that," that Matt initially expressed was a real surprise to me. As the days and weeks went on, the bitterness and anger came out, but on that first evening, it was mostly pity.

I was trying to take this all on board, as was Matt. We just took steps thinking, 'how are we going to deal with this, what do we do?' I know it sounds like I'm repeating, but we felt so lost and unprepared. That's what goes round and round in your head. All the decisions were huge, and it was very muddled with my sister being so involved in the situation too. I didn't know what I wanted to do with my father, but I really wanted to understand him and make sense of it. Matt never wanted to see him again, which I totally understood, but it wasn't so clear cut for me.

266

JANE & MATT'S STORY

My father phoned me at one time and said,

"I really want to talk to you, but I don't know what to say. I can understand how you must be feeling. I'm so sorry... blah, blah, blah..."

It had apparently happened to him when he was younger. Perhaps. It may well have done, and I know it's often the way. Oh, I didn't know what to believe any more. Everything had been put into question and I didn't trust anything he said to me anymore. The only thing was my instinct as a mother, and that's all I had to hang on to.

Clara and I decided we wanted to talk to my father, so we got him to come up to her house. Matt was looking after the children because he didn't want to have anything to do with him. He didn't want to get involved with him directly. My father tried to hide behind absolutely everything when we talked to him. He was in denial about it, well sort of denial. He'd admitted he'd done it, but he was trying to cover everything and not taking any responsibility for it. He even blamed Philippa, saying that she was a "very physical girl." Hello? No don't even go there! She is affectionate, demonstrative, a lovely, loving little girl. Nothing justifies that behaviour towards her. Clara and I had some really strong conversations with him, trying to reason, understand, all of that. You can't understand. He doesn't even understand himself, or know himself. Where does it get you?

I was in this very strange position, really odd, because now I was slap bang in the middle. There's my father here, who's always been my father, but now I don't know who he is. It's like he revealed a mask, that's the only way I could explain it. It's like he's taken off this father mask, and I don't know who this person was. There's my sister here, who is suffering and unearthing all these feelings that she's buried for 30 years, they're all just popping out. I felt awful for her. She had these terrible feelings of guilt, because she felt she could have prevented the situation for Philippa. There's my mother here, who's completely in the dark, has no idea what's going on, her husband who has done this to her daughter and granddaughter, this other stranger as far as I'm concerned. There's my children over here. I'm trying to protect my daughter, primarily. But did it happen to my son? And then there's Matt, who is as lost as I am. We are not armed to deal with this. There were so many facets to it; it was really overwhelming. We tried to take things step-by-step, time went into another void, with the children being the main priority.

JANE & MATT'S STORY

Clara and I decided that the next step would be to have Mum know what was going on. We said to Dad that he had to tell her, because he'd need to explain why he wasn't seeing the grandchildren. She's a loving grandmother, so what did he think she was going to do? Not notice that the grandchildren were no longer coming over? He was saying,

"Oh we're having financial problems, this could be the reason, I'll be able to manage it, get through it. She'll be fine..."

No. Then it was,

"Oh, can't we just leave it, because we're getting on in years, we can't always do the same things..."

No. All of these pathetic excuses.

Matt: All of this was Jane and Clara, not me. I had completely different opinions on the subject - I was not exactly ganged up on, but I was in the distinct minority.

My side of it probably goes a lot further back than Jane's in terms of this distrust of her dad. I never really got on with her dad, and so my feelings were cast a long time before this all came out. It made it clearer for me, what needed to happen, there was no confusion for me, just that I had no audible voice to Jane or her sister.

Jane's dad; I never got on with him because I found him so controlling. I was never going to be good enough for

JANE & MATT'S STORY

his daughter. At first the relationship was like I was the son that he never had, but when we got married and settled down. Well, he didn't exactly change overnight, but this gradual shift to being increasingly controlling of us. When I ran my own company, he would always try to interfere. He had this 'holier than thou' way about him. His way was *always* the best, no matter that I am quite an expert in my field, he just wouldn't have it.

Dinner times were always a time that stuck in my memory, as I would get picked on at the table. Oh it was all very hilarious and funny, but the undertone of it as far as I was concerned was that I was getting bullied. I could have stood up for myself on many occasions, and done a good job of it, but I never did for the sake of a quiet life and for Jane. I bit my tongue for a number of years. I don't know if that was a bad thing or a good thing - but it kept the peace. As time wore on, the relationship just broke down, not to any major extent as it was all bottled up inside of me. Jane says that I am a good judge of character, and he just didn't sit comfortably with me.

I was a little bit angry with Jane for not telling me sooner, but I could understand why she didn't too. I think she was a bit relieved I didn't just pick up my keys and drive around there and try and finish him off. I feel like that sometimes now, but I didn't then. In those first couple of days it was like, I don't know really, but like we were laying the foundations of how we were going to deal with it and him. After those couple of days talking about it, I was very much along the lines of going to the police. I want to go to the police. He'd broken the law, regardless of the fact that this is my daughter, he's broken the law. What he's done is so wrong, so terrible that he should not be a free man. Again, I felt bullied by the family, as I felt I was a stand alone voice, surrounded by this family who wanted to close ranks and just shut the whole thing out, sweep it under the carpet. That's how I felt.

When I first met with Jane and Matt, they had stressed the differences in their stories, and here was the main point of tension. The deep complexity because of the close family relationship between Jane and her father. The degree of distance that Matt had enabled him to think and act more clearly, without the emotional ties of being in the same family.

Both Jane and Matt were able to hold their own feelings and opinions, and at the time, respect the feelings of each other. This is not something that grew with hindsight but was there as events unfolded. This empathy impressed me, and I really believe that this was the vital ingredient that held them together. They often iterated to me about being a team. However, despite there being a team, Jane was the one in control of events. This was her father and she and her sister were trying to push for him taking responsibility for what he had done. I knew that Matt was feeling very differently, but also that he had this ability to contain his feelings, after all he had done so for years with Jane's dad. I wondered how much longer he could contain what he felt. The sexual abuse of his daughter is a very different degree of emotional disquiet.

I commented to Jane that in some ways it would have been easier to deal with a stranger; the tangled feelings of dealing with your own father really inhibited progress, making the situation completely toxic.

Jane: Before you experience anything like this, and you hear about paedophiles, you might say, "lock 'em up," but this is so different. Matt is a very different person, with a different character, but he also has a different dynamic in the relationship, so we dealt with things in such very different ways. Yes, with hindsight, I can see it, how Matt was left out of the way we took it forward. I understood his feelings, but this didn't translate into agreement about how we handled my father. You just don't know how to deal with it. It was so hard for me to adjust to who this person suddenly was. Even though I saw my father very differently, I was so tangled up in how to deal with him.

The next thing was this kind of ultimatum. Clara and I were adamant that he had to tell our mother, but he sidestepped it in so many ways. We phoned him and said,

"We're on the way over, so have you told her?"

"No."

We were minutes away, so he had to tell her. It was awful. When we arrived we were so anxious knowing that Mum was going to be in pieces. He had sat her down, and his words were,

"I have been inappropriate with Philippa..."

That's all he'd said. When we arrived he was sitting in the hallway and she was in the living room, sobbing. We knew we had to take care of her; she saw us, and she was already just sobbing her heart out.

"I can't believe it... Dad's just told me... Oh poor Philippa.... I can't believe I didn't know.... Why didn't I know?... What could I have done, I feel so sorry...."

All of these outcries between sobs, deep heart breaking sobs. And then she looked at us and said,

"Oh God, it didn't happen to either of you two, did it?"

Clara looked at her and said,

"Yes, it happened to me..."

Mum just sobbed more.

Now that Mum knew, we wanted my father to be the one who told the authorities, and Clara and I wanted him to disclose it to the doctor. Clara and I wanted him to get psychiatric help, and we knew that the NHS was the place to access it. This is the start of the situation which brings us to where we are today. They were having these financial difficulties and this ran alongside the abuse. Mum was in such a state, under the doctor, receiving medication to help her deal with things, but the doctor didn't know about the situation with my father. Dad had said that he would talk to the doctor about it, and would go for an appointment, coming back saying that the doctor had sorted it, but nothing changed and we knew he wasn't telling the truth.

Matt: My anger and frustration was building and building. Over this time I felt like a bit of a spare part really; no voice. No matter what I said, it seemed to fall on deaf ears. Again, I can understand the reason for it and where Jane was. Even then, to a certain extent, I was prepared to give him the benefit of doubt when it came to see the doctor, even though he came back and said, "it's sorted." That was a lie. The lies were already forming. He blamed Jane's mum for it because they weren't having a sexual relationship. He blamed Philippa for it, saying that she was a sexual young lady. It was disgusting. All of this was relayed by Jane, because I refused to have anything to do with him. It made me angry as these were not excuses at all for what he'd done, he just couldn't seem to accept that what he did was his fault.

Then out came the line, "I was abused myself at 15..." Well. What did I make of that one? I thought of myself at 15, and at that age I knew the difference between right and wrong, and for me at 15, whomever would have approached me would have met the wrong side of my force - muscles pumped full of testosterone. I took on my own dad at that age. I didn't actually believe it anyway. It doesn't sit comfortably with me when you line it up alongside all the other lies and distractions. If he was, perhaps he was, I don't care. It still doesn't make what he did right, to find a six year old girl sexually arousing.

I went into deep shock with it all. It was like I withdrew, all I could do was go inside of myself to cope with all these raging feelings. One of the saddest things from my point of view was that I felt really uncomfortable having any kind of physical contact with Philippa. Really uncomfortable, because someone had a sexual contact with her. I couldn't bring myself to cuddle her, hold her hand, any touching at all. That carried on for a good eight weeks or so, to the point that it actually harmed our relationship, mine and Philippa's. She picked up on that, and wouldn't come near me either. For me as her father, not to be able to cuddle her before she went to bed, or read to her. It was distressing, really distressing. That was so damaging in itself. It was just time that enabled us to recover that, but over that period it was just dreadful.

The financial problems that emerged just underlined my initial feelings about Jane's father, his ways, and the fact that they'd got themselves into this massive amount of debt. There were more attempts at excuses and he'd now started to play Jane and me off against Clara and her husband, Nick, when all the finances were coming to a head. Nick was pretty astute, and was trying to help them out. He said to me,

"Do you know what he's said?"

"Er, no...."

"He said that they gave you and Jane a big chunk of money and have never asked for it back..."

JANE & MATT'S STORY

Well, this was a complete lie. An old second hand car they gave us, years back, but that does not amount to anything like a great chunk of money. It was another lie. All of these things just making me more, and more, and more angry. I was increasingly adamant that the police should be involved. He was backtracking, making pathetic excuses, using emotional blackmail towards his wife, on the girls. Even then he was still trying to control the situation, trying to control the outcome of where he was trying to lead it. That was just about enough for me. I said to Jane that it was getting beyond a joke and that he was really showing himself to be the person he was, and always had been. Even then, Jane is such a good-hearted person, she was trying to keep everyone happy. I don't think she saw good in him, but she was so allied to her family.

In the meantime, I'd received a letter from him. It was two paragraphs long. Even the grammar in it bugged me.

"I'm sorry for what I done"

It just said to me that he didn't mean it. It was another glib attempt to pass it off. We only found out recently that his wife had made him write it, which didn't come as any great surprise. It wouldn't have made any difference to me if he'd poured his heart out over several pages. He was still wrong for what he'd done and deserved punishment.

I know I've said it before, but I am a 'black and white' kind of person and I do form judgements quickly about people, but in my mind, I do allow people to prove themselves differently. In 18 years he never did, never could. This horrible, horrible mess was underlying perhaps how right I was about him. Things drifted along in this awful space of nothing until he eventually did tell the doctor.

Jane: I was determined that he was going to tell the doctor, but by now I knew that he was not going to actually go and say it very easily. I ended up writing a private and confidential letter to our doctor explaining the situation. I told him that I would accompany my father to the surgery and that I hoped he would impart that he had abused Philippa. I wanted the doctor to be forewarned.

When it was time to go to the doctor, I just so happened to be at the house and I said that I'd walk up with him. I said to my father,

"It is important that you have a chat with the doctor...."

He got defensive and anxious. I said to him,

"I think you need to tell the doctor."

"I'm not gonna go - I'm not gonna go," he replied in a raised voice.

"No, come on, I'll come up with you. I think it's important. I'll sit with you in the surgery. Just have a chat about it."

I knew full well that the doctor knew what was coming, and I was going to make sure we stayed there until he said it.

When we were in front of the doctor. I turned to my father and said,

"I think there's something you've got to tell the doctor. You need to be honest."

He then said the same thing that he said to my mother,

"I've been inappropriate with my granddaughter."

The doctor went with him, gently, and tried to get more information.

This disclosure led to him getting psychiatric help, which is, well, all but pathetic really. Matt all along had been saying that we should go directly to the police, but in telling the doctor, this is where we did end up. The doctor was duty bound to inform social services, and they in turn alerted the police. The doctor phoned me to tell me that this was what was going to happen, and then my father was made aware of it, and he went into panic.

JANE & MATT'S STORY

"I'm going to be put away..."

We were in the hands of the authorities, and we felt that we might finally be getting somewhere.

It had taken about a month from the almost chance revelation by Philippa to get to this point. The route that it took was a very different experience for Jane and Matt, both aching with the pain of what had happened to their daughter. Jane was tied up in the emotional bonds that her family had woven around her over her lifetime, and Matt felt powerless to sever them, helplessly witnessing the slow progress as Jane's father was supported by his family in making his disclosure.

Both Jane and Matt were united in protecting their own children, and had involved the authorities to ensure that Jane's father was no longer a threat to any other child and to seek punishment for his crime.

The next chapter shows how events unfolded, and how their own experiences continued to travel along different paths.

LET DOWN BY THE SYSTEM

Jane: Social services phoned me a day or so later and told me that they had been informed that Philippa had been sexually abused by my father. They said that we were not to let Philippa or Gavin have any contact with their grandfather.

"No, that's fine, there are no worries there." I told them.

They also told me that they had alerted the police.

"OK, fine..."

I had a very tough time here. My mum was so very upset and my father was also in pieces. But you know, all of this had been brought on by himself. It just seemed to go on and on. He had to go down to the police station. He had to do the whole thing. Fingerprints were taken. He was questioned. They made a statement. He had to sign it. My parents were in a mess during this whole period. It was awful.

This is where it started to go downhill, even more so than you think it possibly can do. You know we were not the one bringing charges, or making the prosecution, it's the police, they do this. The Crown Prosecution Service decides when a case can be brought for prosecution. We have no say in it. The police told us that the next step

281

would be to get the facts from Philippa, so that she would need to be interviewed and that one of us would accompany her.

At this point, I interrupted Jane to clarify that it would be a *video* interview.

"No" came back the rapid reply.

I was deeply shocked. This was not something that took place years ago, but around the end of 2007. Through my work at Mosac, I knew about a government wide directive called "Achieving Best Evidence in Criminal Proceedings: Guidance on Interviewing Victims and Witnesses, and Using Special Measures", issued in 2002 and updated in 2007. The guidance specifically requires that where children are giving evidence in sexual offence cases, "video recorded interviews should take place....unless the child objects and/or insurmountable difficulties which prevent the recording taking place (e.g. if the child has been involved in abuse involving video-recording or photography)"[12]

---

[12] 2.77, page 14 in Section 2, Planning and conducting interviews with children in "Achieving Best Evidence in Criminal Proceedings: Guidance on Interviewing Victims and Witnesses, and Using Special Measures" 2007, Criminal Justice System, available as a pdf document.

JANE & MATT'S STORY

I make this point here, not to point a finger at the police force involved, but to bring my experience to bear. It is a case of 'you don't know what you don't know,' and at the time, neither Jane nor Matt knew about interviewing vulnerable witnesses; why should they? There is guidance aimed at obtaining the best evidence, with the welfare of children (and other vulnerable groups) at the heart of horrendous situations like this. Unfortunately, it seems that it was not in place for Philippa.

Jane: No, it was a spoken interview. I wasn't allowed to be present, and I had to wait. There was a female member of social services and a male police officer.

I took Philippa to the police station to be interviewed. I very carefully tried to explain the situation to her, as I had done all along. I told her that they wanted to ask some questions about Granddad.

"Don't worry about it, just be as honest as you can, and tell them what you remember. It's important that they know, so that it doesn't happen again. You'll probably sit in a little room, and a man called Bob will be there asking questions, and a woman called Alice will be there too."

JANE & MATT'S STORY

She was only six. Off she went, as I sat and waited. It was a good three-quarters of an hour.

The police officer, Bob, came down and said that it had taken quite a while for any information to come out of her, which is not surprising, completely understandable. They had managed to get a few facts. So, now they had some facts, they said that they would, oh I can't really remember the timings, but that my father would have to come back. He'd either be called upon, or he could come voluntarily, to respond and make another statement, and perhaps be cautioned. If he didn't come voluntarily he would be arrested. My father decided he would go in voluntarily and answer all the questions that needed to be addressed. So, off he went.

As a result of this he was given a caution, with the consequence that he was placed on the sex offenders register for two years. He also has some restrictions placed on his movements; if he goes away for more than seven days he has to tell the police, and if he moves house, he has to tell the police.

Some time after this, the police phoned us and told us that they wanted to pursue something else. They wanted to place an order on him, a SOPO (Sex Offenders Prevention Order) which would be tailored specifically to him, placing restrictions on him, with contact with minors

JANE & MATT'S STORY

and stuff like that. They went into great detail over the phone - there would be a court appearance, which would only last about 15 minutes, and this is when this order would be issued. We would get our day in court and, with Matt feeling stronger and stronger that this should happen, we could perhaps draw a line under it. There would be some sentence and therefore some punishment.

It all sounded very attractive to us, but in doing so, it was very likely that Philippa would have to have a video interview. We were asked to think about it. We took a good two weeks to really, really think about it. Do we put our daughter through a video interview?

Matt: When things started to go down the route I would have preferred from the outset, now that the police were involved, I was initially relieved. That feeling didn't last very long. I felt the police had this really apathetic approach. There was a real sense of leniency towards him, which didn't sit comfortably with me. Once again my voice was small. The police were doing their job. Even then I started feeling sick to my stomach that he, the perpetrator, was getting all the help. He was the one that seemed to be being treated like the victim. He had help from the doctor, the psychiatrist, the therapist, even the police were giving him choices. All of these people, all rallying around this

285

poor old man who'd done this terrible thing to a child. And we just sat there. Nothing. No one to turn to. No help. Goodness knows we tried. We asked the police if we could get any support,

"Speak to social services," they told us. So we did, we asked social services, and they said,

"Speak to the police...."

They sent us backwards and forwards to each other. Eventually they suggested the GP, so we made another appointment with the GP, only to be told,

"There isn't really anything for you, however, if you start to feel unwell, come back to us and we'll take it from there."

In the meantime the police were doing their thing, not brilliantly, I felt. We have since learnt that they failed to do things properly, like not giving us the choice of having a male or a female police officer interview her. You are in the hands of the authorities, trusting them to do their job in the right way, and you learn they didn't. All of these are the things that make you really mad. I had been waiting for the police to become involved, had really wanted them to throw everything at him, and here we were. It wasn't providing much relief that they were involved. I had wanted much more.

JANE & MATT'S STORY

When the police came back to us, after he'd received this caution, and told us that they wanted to pursue putting a SOPO on him, and that Philippa would have to be interviewed again, but this time by video, it was a really tough call to make. It was such a difficult time for us. We didn't want to put Philippa through it, but at the same time, we wanted him to receive proper punishment. The police said that there was only one way to get anything out of the situation, and that meant that our daughter would have to be interviewed again.

I had the sense from Matt that they were handling this decision differently; it was something they tussled with together, unlike the "what happens to him" about Jane's father. Matt reflected, and replied.

Matt: Yes, absolutely. It was different. This was about *our* daughter, rather than about Jane's father. It made it clearer in some ways. I think that Jane was less keen on the idea of Philippa being interviewed again than I was, but it was something we worked through together. We took a couple of weeks to decide. It was at our pace, which was helpful. We weren't under any pressure to come to a decision quickly. We decided that we would go ahead, and we would be able to get a day in court. You have to recognise that by now it was a few months on, and we were getting desperate to move on.

Jane: From my perspective, it was somehow the right thing to be doing for justice. The order needed to be done, and Philippa had to be interviewed for that. It wasn't a good thing to do, it wasn't an ideal thing to do, but it was the right thing to do.

A time was set up for her to do this video interview. Again, we very carefully talked to her about it and explained it as best we could. That it would be the same man, Bob, but a different lady. We explained it carefully, just so that she could know what was going to happen, trying to go through it in the simplest of ways. We said that when it was done, we'd all go and do something nice like have coffee and cake.

Matt: We both went with her on this occasion. It was awful just going there, knowing what was going to happen. We weren't allowed to go in with her, because we couldn't risk leading the witness, so we had to wait outside, which was so, so hard.

When Philippa came out she was so quiet. It had taken them a long time to get anything out of her, but what do you expect? She was only six at the time, and as far as she was aware, she was getting Granddad into trouble. So really and truly, it was horrible for her. She wasn't as bad, as upset, as we'd expected her to be. We got into the car and said,

"Right, shall we go and have cake?" and she said,

"Yeaaaah!"

We'd already planned to try to lighten the situation. Within the hour she seemed to be more chuffed about having chocolate cake with just Mummy and Daddy and not being in school. However, Jane and I were still really cut up about it.

After the interview, Philippa was taken into another room with a female police officer and the female social worker whilst Jane and I spoke to the male interviewing officer, Bob. I got quite tearful then; I was hearing this middle aged man using words that could only have come from my daughter's mouth. Names for certain parts of the body, and stuff like that. Bob told us that on at least one occasion there was a wet patch on her leg. That can only mean one thing, which bothers me to this day. He's not admitted to that, so I'll never know. I will never ever know. For the rest of that day, I was in pieces really. I know that men are supposed to be big and strong, but I felt really fragile, I'm not sure what the expression is, just really small and meek. And wounded. I was quite deeply hurt and needing to know more. There was also another part of me that knew I may never know what really happened, and he's not going to admit to anything that can't be proven. If we'd have known at the time, we'd have made sure her tights weren't washed, but we had no idea. Those are the kind of things that trap you. I'd started getting lower and lower and it was starting to affect my work. Work were aware of what was going on - my MD, direct line manager and HR manager. All were very supportive. Any amount of time I needed, it was mine. They even sent me home on a couple of occasions when key things were going on with the police; they told me to go home and be with Jane. Going to work was my escape, I could lose myself, albeit not performing to the full of my ability, but it was a break from it. Work was a safe space for me.

The agony of making a decision to subject your daughter to another rigorous interview was something that Jane and

JANE & MATT'S STORY

Matt struggled with. It is so tough that justice can only be handed out by involving child victims. They had wrestled with the decision, and I was hopeful that they would be rewarded. I was not prepared for what happened next.

Jane: It was a few weeks later when the phone rang, and I picked it up to Bob, the police officer. I assumed it was a call to let us know how they were going on, well, it was in some way I guess, but I never expected what he was about to say to me,

"Just to let you know, we can't continue with the order."

"What?"

"We've been advised by our legal team that we are unable to proceed with the order, as your father was cautioned when he came in, we are unable to place an order on him."

I could not believe it, it was horrendous. It felt like everything was caving in and we were being left with nothing. When I told Matt, he just fell apart.

Matt: I was so angry. Absolutely furious. I wanted to hear it for myself, so I phoned up the police and said,

"What do you mean, you're not pursuing this?" The response felt so blasé to me,

"Well, as we've cautioned him, he cannot be tried and punished for something that he has already been punished for."

"What do you mean, can't be punished? Does that mean the caution counts as a punishment?"

"Yes."

"What do you mean, a case of double jeopardy?"

"Yes, effectively."

"Who is responsible for this? This is not acceptable."

"Give me a couple of hours and I'll call you back."

He didn't call back, so I ended up phoning back later that day. They were pointing the finger at their legal department in HQ as being the ones who said they could go for a trial, and it had been their Superintendent going for this SOPO. It doesn't really matter who got it wrong; they did. I just couldn't understand why they allowed this to happen, make our daughter go through this video interview process when the oldest law in the land says you can't do this. Why did no one pick it up? Unfortunately the person dealing with it in the legal department has now left. For God's sake! I got so angry with them for this. I wasn't rude - I didn't swear or bawl but I made it clear that it wasn't the last of it.

JANE & MATT'S STORY

Jane: I couldn't get my head around it. It was devastating to us. We'd built Philippa up to doing this. We had thought so carefully about the wisdom of putting her through it. We took our time. Was it the right thing to do, was it going to help? Not at all, so it seems. All of those things you do with such trepidation because it's your child, your vulnerable child, being put in this position through no fault of her own. We are in this awful position through no fault of our own. What do you do? Where can you go next?

I was deeply shocked when I heard how they had been let down. When Jane was telling me the story for the first time, when she said that the police could not proceed with the SOPO, double jeopardy flashed in my mind. It is blindingly obvious when you are one step removed from their story, and it makes sense to them both with hindsight. However, when you're in the thick of this utter horror, it isn't obvious. It isn't as if Jane and Matt were rushed into a decision, there was plenty of time for the reality to be presented, only it wasn't.

How can a caution be just punishment? It makes no sense to me. I have certainly learnt a lot about the criminal justice system second hand in meeting the parents and carers of children who have been sexually abused. One thing that strikes me about all the individuals is how much trust and faith they give to the authorities, and how often they come to regret that. I wish that I could write it differently.

Jane and Matt were left reeling from their experience, and had to try to pick up the pieces and find another path through this, since justice had been denied them.

Jane: As I said, Matt really suffered; he gradually got really ill over the way things continued. I know looking back it was all tied up with how I was with my family, my mum and my dad, but I just didn't see it until it got almost too late.

I was trying to accommodate everybody, as I have always done. Even though my father has committed this terrible crime I am trying to accommodate him. I'm trying to accommodate my mother and make sure that she's all right. I'm trying to get everyone to keep speaking to each other, trying to make everything better, but it's not going to be better. Eventually I realised that Matt was getting more and more upset because I was taking our children over to see my parents. One day, I finally thought, 'what am I doing?'

Matt: Yes, things were getting worse and worse for me. It was a kind of descent on this very slippery slope. I was getting very depressed and not feeling very well at all. I went back to the doctor and he referred me to a psychiatrist. I really thought I was going to finally get some help with all of this, so I went along for this appointment. About the third question she asked was,

"Are you feeling suicidal?"

"No," I replied.

"Well, there's not a lot we can do for you then. Take these tablets."

I was handed a prescription, which I was not interested in taking. I didn't want to take any pills, I wanted some help. So, you're not suicidal, you're fine. It was like a box had been ticked and I was back out, alone.

It was getting towards the end of June, which is when Jane's father's birthday is. Jane's mum had invited our children over to the house to celebrate his birthday. She had said to Jane,

"If you won't do it for him, do it for me...."

I had said to Jane five or six times in the week leading up to his birthday,

"Look, I don't want the kids to go."

She said to me,

"What can I do? Mum's asking me..."

"I don't want Philippa setting foot in that house again, and I don't want him seeing them again, supervised or not. I just don't want it."

I was getting more and more worked up about it; they were going there on his birthday. The day comes and I was taking Gavin to a football tournament and Jane took Philippa up to their house for his birthday. I'd worked myself into such a real state, it was just awful. It took effect a couple of days later when I had to go up to London to a meeting. I didn't feel right and I actually collapsed in St John's Square in London. I don't remember much about it. I recall coming to in an ambulance, with an oxygen mask strapped to my face. It's a real haze. I hadn't slept more than $1^{1/2}$-2 hours a night for the previous six weeks, so I was physically exhausted, mentally exhausted and very anxious. It had all caught up with me and 'bang', there I went. My body had had enough. I finally got some help from the doctor - I was seen and taken seriously. He prescribed some medication, which I'm still taking now. I had about three weeks off work, but the prize was that Jane really saw how upset I had been about this visit. She decided there and then, "that's it. He is not going to see our children. They are not going there."

Jane: Yes, it was like something inside me just clicked. I think it was seeing Matt so ill with it that was the trigger, and I just thought, 'I've got to be thinking about my family, I can't keep thinking about them, I have got to think about *my* family. My immediate family. What am I doing?' So there was this big realisation in me, so I did say to Matt,

"That's it, there's no contact. It ends between my father and the children..."

I went over there and had a conversation with my mother - I couldn't even speak to him; I didn't know what to say to him anymore. I told her I was sorry that the relationship was ending but that it was wrecking us.

"I can't have the children seeing him and that's the way it's going to be until they reach an age when they can make a decision for themselves."

It's like I have to do it now for their protection. That's the way it's been for the last year or so. My mum was upset, but she did say she understood why we had to do this.

JANE & MATT'S STORY

It is not an uncommon experience that events often have to take a dramatic turn before change can take place. It seems that Matt's body breaking down communicated to Jane the extent of his pain and it freed her from the bonds of her own family. With Jane taking a stance for her family, perhaps they could move on? The next chapter explores the impact that it has had on their family and raises the issue of loyalty as Jane's mother still lives with the abuser, her husband.

STRUGGLING ON

Jane: About a year ago we began our work with Mosac, which was a complete chance encounter. After Matt had his breakdown, we decided that we needed some proper support to help us deal with all of this. We wanted specialist help, from people who had experience and understanding of our situation, we wanted counselling for us so that we could be strong for our children. Matt did loads of research and came up with nothing. We searched everything locally; nothing. Then Matt was talking to somebody at his work about it, and her mother was a psychotherapist, and she'd relayed the story back to her mother,

"You need to speak to Mosac," came the response the very next day.

We made contact with Mosac and went for an assessment. We really wanted help together, and fortunately Mosac were able to offer us this. Thank God they did, because I don't know where we'd be without it. For seven or eight months we had floundered around on our own, but finally we were being given the support we'd been desperately in search of.

JANE & MATT'S STORY

Matt: We saw our counsellor at Mosac, and then we went away for two weeks on holiday. It was our first two-week break since our honeymoon some 14 years previously. It was just at the right time. I'd gone back to work part-time for three days and then we had this holiday booked. That holiday was the saving of me personally because I was able to step away from all of this mire, allow the medication to properly kick in and achieve some kind of balance. It was fantastic. I felt relaxed for the first time in, well, many years to be honest. It was really healing.

We came back and started the counselling in earnest. I cannot stress enough how it was the saving of me, personally, and how much it helped us deal with the things around us. Just having that supportive understanding of someone who knows what this might be feeling like. Our counsellor was very intuitive, and she really helped us navigate through this whole mess.

Jane: We were really guided through by Mosac. We felt a great need to speak every Friday afternoon. Every week we came out and felt, what's the word? 'good' about talking about it. There were many different facets, concentrating on different things each week as situations arose. We were able to relate to our counsellor, and she would help us explore the best way to deal with it, offering amazing insights. It was really important as we felt we were floundering in the dark. Her experience and intuitive mind has so helped us.

Matt: Yes, it saved me from either being behind bars or six feet under. It really has, because I've never experienced real anger in my life before all of this. I'm a real pacifist. I've always been the least angry person that any of my friends have known; the least aggressive. The first sign of trouble and I'm off! Sure I can handle myself, but I don't choose to as I'd rather talk things through. I've played American football and rugby, but that's sport - the moment you put a gum shield on you're a different person. The anger I experienced was so toxic, I was getting angry with myself for feeling angry and it was building and building. This real rage all going inwards as I wasn't taking it out on anybody else. I was having major problems sleeping.

With Mosac's help, I was able to get my point across to Jane that I was *really* feeling bad about this. I wasn't giving her ultimatums as I really felt for her position, and I really wanted to understand her. At the same time, I wanted Jane to see how wrong it all was, and our counsellor was so helpful in that process. She didn't take sides in any way, but she helped us both understand each other's point of view. Each time we went to Mosac we came back having taken another step forwards. Each week there was something we could talk about, having a problem to look at, and each week we felt we were resolving things more. That in itself was a massive help. Like stepping stones across a massive river. I still only think we're about half way across, but we're armed now. We know we can now deal with these things on our own, and we no longer need others' help to deal with it.

Jane: It's so ironic that we nearly didn't get this help. There should be something like this in every county. We'd love to champion for it. Not because you *want* to believe that child sexual abuse is prevalent, but because it *is*. It *does* happen, there are no two ways about it. It happened to us so we now know. It is going to happen to many more people. If there were lots of Mosac's you'd sleep better in your bed knowing that there's the right help out there. Unfortunately, as we found, there are bits of services. The doctor can help with one thing, the community psychiatric nurse another, but the help offered by Mosac is so specialist. They really believed in us being the ones who could make the difference to our children, and the focus was on us. The frontline support for Philippa was there, which must be a priority, but there must be something for the parents and carers too.

JANE & MATT'S STORY

This view is no surprise to me, as I hear it from most clients in my own work at Mosac. We have a catalogue of testimonies to this effect in the files in the office. I know how valuable it is as a lifeline to parents and carers. I often feel that we are an anchor holding a client on a stormy sea. The sea is relentless, as wave upon wave continues to batter. Recovery is a long journey. Jane and Matt know from their own experience that everything is affected, and that every day living becomes challenging with constant decisions about who to tell or not to tell.

Jane: Yes, every day there is something. Some days you feel like walking down the road and you want to scream it from the rooftops.

"This is what happened! My father did this! Look at my poor child!"

All these things you want to shout and tell everyone. There are bad people around and everyone has to be warned. Then, on other days, you want to hide away because you think that people might know what has happened, and that it's my father who did it. The shame of it. All these different feelings.

JANE & MATT'S STORY

Ultimately, we've been very careful about who we've told. Some people we've instinctively felt aren't the right people to tell, so we haven't. We talked about this with our counsellor, and we've really trusted our instincts. We have told some people, the parents of our children's best friends. We get on really well with them, but we wanted the support network to exist beyond just us two. It's such a strange line because you don't want it to be a taboo, but you also want it to be supportive for the children. You want to throw a protective shield around them, but that's so hard to do. They've both been affected by it, it's not just Philippa who has been affected.

Gavin went through a really difficult time with it. My father had said that he didn't do anything to Gavin, but of course we didn't believe him so we had to speak to Gavin about it. Also, not seeing your granddad, you have to be able to explain it, and we've always been truthful with our children. We had to try to find the right words to ask Gavin, the right things to say to him. It was awful. Gavin assured us that nothing had happened, nor that he'd been under any pressure from him. He has really struggled with it. Gavin's like Matt, a real thinker, and like me too. I mull things over and look for the answers, so between those two processes, Gavin's been struggling with how to deal with it.

JANE & MATT'S STORY

At one level he's grieving for his grandfather - he hasn't seen him and doesn't know if he's going to see him again. Then there are these questions, "why did it happen?" "what happened?" and "why did it happen to Philippa?" All these questions which we've had to go through with him. We've had many, many conversations with him.

Gavin was getting really upset, and struggling to cope at school and with his friends. We spoke to the school about it, and they jumped on it straight away. They were just brilliant. We were referred to CAMHS[13] who provided a counsellor for Gavin. He has been fantastic. He has really helped Gavin come through it. As much as we could talk to him and try to explore things, Gavin really needed someone outside of the situation to help him. We kept saying it was OK to feel these things - upset because you're not seeing Granddad, confused because of all these questions, angry because of it. We told him we were feeling them too, and that we couldn't understand it. We had to be honest and say to him,

"Actually, we can't make sense of it either."

As a parent you feel you should be able to answer your child's questions. He's such a bright boy, and he needed some things sorting out before he could move on.

---

[13] See footnote 8

CAMHS have helped him so much to do that. Occasionally there's a little blip and he gets upset, but he's really doing well now.

More recently, I had a conversation with Gavin about sexual relationships. He'd been talking about sex education in class, so it was raised in his mind, again. I had to put it in the context that a healthy sexual relationship was this, and the situation with Granddad was not healthy. It is hard, because you want to speak about the positives in a sexual relationship, and not have him disturbed by sex as he grows up. It upsets me that they are dealing with adult issues when they are still only children.

Philippa has dealt with it in a very different way. She's just sailed through it, not really having any thoughts about it. She's just got on with it. She didn't seem to get upset with the police interviews. I imagine she's just put away in a little box, because it's too confusing to deal with. It's going to come out at some point, for sure. Both of us think that there will come a time when it will affect her, and she'll, well, whatever. In a way, I hope it does come out and that she's able to talk about it, and we're able to tell her it was wrong. We're alert to this. You don't want to keep on raising it in case that adds to anything, but we're alert to it. The school knows, the doctor knows. We have to just trust that we know our daughter.

The thing that makes it live for me is the situation with my mum. She is still living with my father, and until that changes, it's impossible to move on. Almost two years since it all came out, she's still there. She cries herself to sleep at night, so she cannot be happy. She's been with him for over 45 years and doesn't know how to escape. She's been in this controlling, abusive relationship for so long that she just doesn't know anything else. She is so dependent on him - she doesn't drive and things just orbit around him.

I've been on many walks with her, had many conversation with her about it. I've said that if she needs help, if she needs someone, if she wakes up one day and she doesn't want to be there then I will, we will, help. It's not my place to tell her what to do; it's not my decision, but hers. If she stays with him, then there are conditions. Unfortunately, that's how it has to be. If she decides to walk away, I'll be there immediately. I'd go with her to the Citizen's Advice Bureau to help her work out the money side of things. We would do whatever we could to help her, we've both said it. Unfortunately, as long as she's with him, she makes it very difficult. She's not facing up to the reality of it and she's in limbo. She has only told one of her friends about it because she wants to keep this facade that everything is the same.

I've tried talking to her, and she says she's not happy. I tell her that she's got the rest of her life to lead. I think she could be so much more than she is and much happier. It sounds like blackmail when you say it, but it's the way it has to be. I am a forgiving person, but I cannot bring myself to forgive him. I just can't. I don't think I ever will because I just don't understand it. It's a horrible situation, because of him. He has broken this family. My sister and I get on very well now, better than we did, but my relationship with my mum is not what it was. As long as she stays with him, we are locked in this limbo together. It is purgatory.

Matt: This situation with Jane's mum is really getting to me. The way I see it is she isn't showing us any loyalty. She says she loves us and her grandchildren but she isn't showing it by supporting him, the man that has sexually abused her own child and her grandchild. I just don't get it.

I have a real problem with double standards, and Jane's mum is living this out. The kids were going to spend a day with their grandma, which I didn't approve of, and I found myself getting more and more wound up about it as the day was getting closer. I was really anxious, nauseous and I could feel myself dissociating from myself again. To me it's just wrong. I don't think Jane realises quite how bothered about it I am. I know that's because I don't lay it out - largely because I don't want her to be under any more pressure than she already is. She is under enormous pressure at the moment. It's just that every time it's wearing me down and down and down. Just as I think I'm getting a little better, something else crops up. I was diagnosed with PTSD[14], which is just a label at the end of the day. As far as I'm concerned that's what soldiers get in war zones, it's not me. It's a label that's all too often used. I know there's something wrong but whether it's that, I don't know. I remain a little sceptical. I recognise there's something wrong, because I feel bad. I am in a situation again where I felt helpless and I don't cope well with it.

As callous as it sounds, if it were my parents I'd have no problem with turning round and saying to them,

"Fuck off; never darken my door again. I don't want to know you any more."

I know Jane can't do that, but I also know if it were the other way around, I'd have no problem casting them off. I know Jane is a different person, and she feels very differently. I also know she's torn apart by it all. In its

---

[14] PTSD, Post Traumatic Stress Disorder, is diagnosable psychological and physical condition

own way, it comes with its own set of stresses, worries and problems. Again, as much as I try to understand that, I find it very difficult to, because as far as I'm concerned, if Jane's mum is still with him, then she's sharing his problem.

I know there's a degree of embarrassment that Jane's mum feels about it, which is her materialistic side - I call her the "Queen of Baker Street" because of the way that things have to be, all nice and prim and proper. Yet she's shacked up with a criminal - not any kind of criminal but a paedophile. In my view the loyalty she shows him is so misplaced, and until she makes that break, as far as I'm concerned, she shouldn't be having contact with us. And yes, it's blackmail, there's no other word for it.

Matt's position cannot be misconstrued as you hear him speak. He turns to Jane and apologises, not for his feelings, but for the burden it places on Jane. It seems an impossible position to be in, and it strikes me that there are many other stories in this 'life experience,' because here we are at a hint of another, Jane's mum. I am feeling caught, because there are no right ways in all of this, and the strain on life today is evident. Matt is true to his word at not wanting Jane to suffer the burden of this alone. When I am at their house, the phone rings and Matt answers. It is Jane's mother on the phone. Matt is polite, but brief in relaying a message. The timing is incredible, as Matt was telling me of his pain because of her inaction before she called. I marvel at his composure which he tells me is for Jane's sake. His sacrifice touched me, and I hope that they are offered a way through this very soon.

In this exchange, Jane acknowledges Matt's apology, and goes on to explore the impact her mother remaining with her dad has had on her.

Jane: Matt needn't be sorry, he shouldn't be sorry. There are many things I agree with, it's just so difficult. A lot of the emotions he feels, I feel too. I am so frustrated with my mum's indecision, her lack of making a choice. Initially I gave her the benefit of the doubt as she was going through such a tough time, taking it all on board. Now? I just don't understand her. After all this time of reflection and sadness, a sadness that is permanently with her, why doesn't she just choose to go? There is something binding her to him. Something, his control perhaps? She's said to me on many occasions that she'd be able to do things, have independence in a new life, but that she just can't find the strength to go. She knows everything he's done, she's talked about it, so she does know what he's done.

For me, I just can't understand. What does it take for someone to get up and go? It's almost like, I know, it's likening it to someone who's alcoholic, but it's like some kind of addiction. She can't see it. She's in denial about it, she must be, because if she truly thought about it, she'd see how it upsets us, day in, day out, week in, week out.

We had a meeting in here with my sister only a couple of months ago, when Gavin was going through a really tough time. Mum sat there and sobbed the whole time as I was telling her about how it had affected Gavin. She sat there and said that if this was how it was going to be for us, then she'd have to leave him. She said that here, and she's still there. She sobbed when we had our business launch; when we got in the car to leave, she cried because my father wasn't there. It's the 'what was' that she's struggling with, I think. She's sobbing for what she's lost rather than what is there around her. It's not truly, truly here and now. It's not where the damage is. We, us, the children, we are all suffering. I'll have to have that conversation with her again soon, because this in-between isn't helping us at all.

She sat here before last Christmas and said to us,

"Do you not think he's been punished enough?"

I just said, "No. Absolutely not."

It's because he's not seeing his grandchildren. Well, what does he expect? He doesn't see me so he's lost one daughter, and he only vaguely sees my sister and that's the one he's abused. There is an allegiance to him after all of this, and we just don't understand it. She's from a different generation, era. It doesn't justify it, but it's the only way that I can try to understand it, even though I don't, really I don't.

Mum can't value herself very much. I know she didn't have a great start in life, with her own traumas, and in my father she found someone who's given her a sense of something. However, that's been put under a great big question mark, but it's not enough for her to think, 'Right, that's it! I'm going to have to be here for the rest of my family.' There is something that keeps her there. What does he have to do? What else is he capable of? The mistrust, betrayal, abhorrence, still doesn't make her go "Enough!" We've said to her that we'd help her if she wants to leave, but the decision has to be made by her. It's like she's almost come to this place where she goes, "my life is sort of easier, because I am putting up with him. It's OK."

But Mum, you're not happy.

Matt: I wrote a seven-page letter to Jane's mum before Christmas last year. It was from my heart, pouring out my feelings to her, because I don't see her much. It took me a month to write it; for it to say what I wanted to convey. It was honest and open, some of it good and some of it bad. The first thing she did with it was show it to him. Apparently he turned to her and said,

"that's it, you're definitely going to leave me now, aren't you?"

Such manipulation. She came over to see us, and she said to me,

"I don't understand why you've written me this letter. Seven pages. Why write to me and not to Jane's dad?"

Uh? Why would I write to him? I don't give a damn about him! She missed the point completely.

Jane: Matt wrote to her because he cares about her. You wouldn't write that to someone you don't care about. She just doesn't get it. Matt spent ages thinking so carefully about what he wanted to say to her, and she just can't see it's her he cares about.

Matt: I want her to have a full and complete relationship with her grandchildren, and I want them to have a full and

JANE & MATT'S STORY

complete relationship with their grandmother. It's not going to happen as long as she lives with him, condoning what he's done and keeping it all a big secret. Her loyalties are with him, so that's what she chooses. She betrays us. She's living this miserable existence because it's habit, nothing else. Forty-five years of marriage is a long time, but it's built on such a deep betrayal and lies.

Jane: My own upbringing. I look back on it now and think that it was a lie, some of it, but it feels so tarnished. The hardest thing is to think, see, feel that something was a lie, tarnished with bad. It is so hard to come to terms with. I have made the best of it, but somehow my mum at 70 is thinking, 'Well, I haven't got much life ahead of me.' But there is so much more. She is *only* 70. It's an easy life, uncomfortable, but easy. It's familiar to her.

None of us are satisfied with this horrible situation. It's a horrible compromise she's making. It's not even a compromise; it's too muddy. It's not enough for us to move on. The prospect of her not doing anything, which means her not seeing our children, hurts me, it really hurts me.

I met her this week, and it was quite a significant conversation. I don't see her that often, not only because we're so very busy, but because it's just so difficult. The more I meet her, the more difficult it is. We have very

315

similar conversations, with no particular outcomes and no resolution. It's a complete limbo situation.

"At this moment…"

She's said it a number of times, she is staying there. She said she's packed her bags before now, and unpacked them. She just cannot imagine life without him. I don't know if she means it, but "at the moment" came up repeatedly. It feels different, but I'm not sure if I'm just looking for confirmation that she will leave him.

This seems to be the trap that they are caught in. The family is desperate to be able to move on, but they are unable to. The shadow of the abuse lives around them every day, as Jane's mum struggles to take any action. She is caught in her own story and for now, seems unable to right herself. Jane is right, it feels very muddy.

There are many lives tied together in this story of Philippa's abuse, and as Jane and Matt tell their stories, we can see the impact that it has on not only them, but others too. Gavin has been deeply affected by it, and we have hints of how it has had an impact on Jane's mum through the comments made by both Jane and Matt.

JANE & MATT'S STORY

The final chapter in their story examines the effect that it has had on them, as individuals, as parents, and what sense they have made when they reflect on it.

FINDING HOPE

You cannot help but be affected by such life events, and Jane and Matt have almost made it their mission to deal with it upfront and not brush the experience away. They have sought to air and share their differences, in the belief that it would have the best possible impact on their family.

When I went back to speak to Jane and Matt, after they had given me their story, they gave more reflections, exploring how it has affected them. In hoping that it might help you, reader, this is where their experiences take us now. Matt begins by reflecting how they handled the differences they had.

Matt: As you know, in the early days there were a lot of conflicting views. Not a conflict *between* us, but a major, major difference of opinion. It was literally black or white in terms of what should have happened. I'm still very adamant about some things and Jane has a completely opposite view. We just live with that. Unfortunately most of the differences there is no right or wrong with no

318

possibility of a compromise because one or the other of us is going to be feeling it wasn't right for them.

Jane: Yes. It was mostly a difference of opinion, Matt's right. We still have different approaches now, as we deal with things differently. There's been moments when that's been really useful too. I've had moments when I've really fallen down, and he's been there to pick me up, and vice versa. At the very crux of it, our main focus has always been the children. It's been what to do for the best for the children. With Matt there's no vested interest in it at all; it's a member of my family and there's still some members of my family I want to maintain a relationship with. My mother. However, it's so frustrating because any conversation with her is so difficult. It's not the relationship that I want with my mother, as it's all tarnished talking about this situation.

If we could start moving away from it, goodness! I don't see my father anyway, but I've said to my mum that I will not have a relationship with him. She doesn't try to influence me anymore with that, which is a change, I guess. She's coming to terms with my feelings, but she's got some way to go with her own.

JANE & MATT'S STORY

I am struck how Jane has changed as a daughter, and I am curious to hear how they perceive they've changed as individuals and as parents.

Jane: I have definitely changed as a person as a result of this. The counselling helped me hugely. I was able to see how I was in this whole process, it's made me realise who I am. It sounds a bit trite, but actually, growing up, I always felt I had to have permission to do everything, and I never felt I was doing the right thing. There were times when I felt I was trying too hard to make it right. I was always trying to make things right. So when this all started, that's what I was trying to do. Make things right. So when I couldn't make it right, it was so tough for me.

The counselling really helped me see how I was, and how I could be different. I'm much more assertive now, and less trapped by how I was raised to be. I didn't see how much things were soothed in my family, growing up. I really think I've changed enormously since this all came up because I've come away from it, their influences. I have really found myself. I've always felt an underlying pressure that things have got to be, 'just so,' you know, do it like this. I've been trying to punch my way out of it, and now I have, it feels odd, but it makes sense. I feel freedom and confidence where I never had it before. I always felt this shadow over me, and now that's gone. I feel empowered because I don't feel associated with this person who has controlled me all my life.

I am also more cynical towards other people, which is horrid. You have this mistrust of people. I try to keep it in perspective, because not everybody wants to abuse children, but I look at older men in a very different light, and that's awful. Really, honestly, I look at a particular generation with suspicion. It's really horrible. I feel in my mind I'm tarring everybody with the same brush. I look and think, 'are you a paedophile?' It's not nice, because I have never been that kind of person, I always wanted to see the best in people, and now I can't, not with his generation.

I'm not sure if it's affected me as a parent. I have changed as an individual, but has that had an impact on me as a parent? I'm not sure. I always felt strength as a parent. Even in the times of despair, I still had a conviction that Matt and I would be able to deal with it. I've always believed we're strong parents, and that conviction has stayed throughout.

Matt: I'd agree with Jane. She's not changed as a parent, she's been so strong throughout this for our children. I don't think she feels the same sense of failure as a parent, as I do. I've changed massively as a parent, but not so much as an individual.

I now place much more emphasis on my family, and I'm much more careful with them when we're larking around and things like that. It's a real negative in my book, because I check myself with them, and I really don't want to be like that. I'm also worried that I'll end up being an overly strict dad, which I'm worried about. I'm fearful of how I might be going forward. I want to be a 'cool dad' not some 'strict no-fun dad.'

I am more ferociously protective of them - more aware of the lengths that I'd go to protect them. This is because I feel I've failed as a father. I carry this with me every day, I failed to protect my daughter. I've not done my job because I wasn't there to protect my little girl from something terrible. My head tells me I shouldn't feel guilty about it, but my heart can't agree on that matter. That's something that has broken me and shattered me, that inability to do my job. Whatever job I've done, I've given my all, and this is the one job I haven't done properly. I don't like failure - I don't like it one bit. It's not a nice feeling to get up every morning and look at myself in the mirror and say, "That's my little girl over there, and she's been hurt, she's been exposed to things she shouldn't have been."

I'd do anything to turn back the clock, but I can't, so I'll do anything to make sure that it doesn't happen again.

Like other stories within this book, the sense of injustice is very live in both of them. Jane and Matt feel very let down by the police, and I wonder how a sense of justice might be restored to them, given that a custodial sentence has been denied.

Matt: If we could turn back the clock, that might help, but in the absence of that? I would love to have two years of our lives back. I would so love to know he's behind bars, but because of the spectacular cock-up by the police, well, I'm not sure. We feel so let down, and there were mistakes. One day, when I have the strength and energy to deal with it, I will pursue them. I know we don't stand a chance, but I have to try. Maybe one day. Even if we get it publicised, it might help somebody else. Justice doesn't seem ours to have, but it will be better for me knowing he's buried in the ground.

Jane: I would love it that others would be more aware of what might happen. We had no idea about the police, courts, anything like that before all of this. You're going through so many things connected with the trauma of what's happened to your child, and you have no idea of what you should be doing in the eyes of the law. What are you entitled to? What's the process? We had no legal advice and, with hindsight, maybe we should have done. You trust the police when you step into the police station. We put our trust in them to do their job properly, and they really let us down.

It makes you feel more shattered because you're already feeling crap because you've let your child down, you've failed as parents, all of these feelings. The one group of people you want to do their job don't. It just adds to the stress. Where else can you go? Fortunately we managed the steep climb with the help of Mosac.

I know that Mosac has been a lifeline to Jane and Matt. I also know that the service will not be available to some readers, and therefore I ask them where else they found support.

Matt: Nowhere else. Really, no.

Jane: I did a lot of research in the early days looking for support. We had pockets of support in places. Like the school, we told them so that they could care for our children. The doctor was very caring, but there was no support as such. Nothing that they could do to really help us. We did have a couple of really good friends, which was fantastic, but at times you just wanted someone who knew what path you were on. We needed the professional, expert help that Mosac provided. Friends, the doctor, they don't have the wherewithal to deal with it. A friend isn't trained in that, and neither is the GP.

Matt: Ah, but a child abuser gets all sorts of support. The victim can get support, but us in the middle? We have nothing. I am so bitter about this.

325

JANE & MATT'S STORY

It is understandable to be bitter, particularly when you hear of how Jane and Matt felt so abandoned by the statutory systems around them. I wondered what advice they would give to a non-abusing parent or carer dealing with the sexual abuse of their child.

Jane: Find a friend that you can talk to. If it's a couple you can both talk to, together or individually, it doesn't matter, but try and find someone. Instinctively we knew who we thought would be there for us, and be able to handle us as non-judgmentally as they could. This is such an emotive, controversial subject. It's so unknown, so you need someone who can try to help with all of that. It also should be someone outside of the family situation, if it is a family. You need the objectivity. The professional help was invaluable, but I also needed help that I could just call on. Someone to go and have a coffee with. You do feel alone in not knowing how to deal with it. Being a parent is like being in the dark at the best of times, but this was something else. This major thing has happened to us as parents, and it's affected so many people. It is so traumatic. You have to talk about it. To close yourself up and try to deal with it alone isn't the path to follow, because I think you'd just completely implode with it.

Matt: My advice would be to call Mosac before you do anything! Then call the police so that you can make sure that things are done properly. We were so helpless with the police. But Mosac and the police! Well!

Jane: That would have been great!

Matt: The other thing is to completely stuff your family — get your priorities right from the very start. Never sweep it under the carpet. Jane's family tried to in the beginning, but you just shouldn't do that.

Jane: It's not the thing to do to keep it quiet. Not the way. It's not only about right or wrong but you want your child to be able to express themselves freely and not become some deep-seated trauma. If you can give them space to deal with it openly, then you hope they can recover.

Matt: Mosac first to help you ensure that things are done properly. They can give you a pathway. We were the ones telling people about them though. The police, the doctors, the social services. The only person we came across who'd heard of them was Gavin's counsellor at CAMHS. It shouldn't be that way around when you're desperately looking for help.

Jane: It's something our country doesn't do very well, take a whole view. There are always policies when things have happened, and they deal with bits of things. It is rare to look at things as a whole. Philippa's abuse was the same. They deal with her, rightly so, they deal with the perpetrator, but if it were a whole, they'd consider us too. It stands to reason that if we're getting help, then we can better help our child.

Jane and Matt are passionate about the professional support they received from Mosac, and as someone involved in the charity, I can't be objective. Parents/carers are out there who do manage without the loving arms that Mosac seeks to embrace its clients with, but Jane makes an interesting point. Why should it be a fringe service available only to some? Jane and Matt tell me that they will campaign going forward; I think they have made the greatest contribution in giving their stories to this book.

JANE & MATT'S STORY

I also want to give Jane and Matt a chance to reflect on any positives that have emerged from the situation, focussing not only on the shadows that they lived with, but also the light. Where did they find hope?

Matt: Me; I found my family again. My life had been work until that point, and it's terrible that it takes something like this to happen, but it helped me see what was really important in life. My source of hope is the three people that live under this roof with me. That's as simple as it can get. In the last two years nothing else has really mattered to me and they give me hope. I've found new ways of loving my family, of showing them how much I care. The downside of all of that is that I've been massively unwell. It's had a physical, emotional and mental cost but I do feel stronger love for my family than I ever have. I don't just mean the kids, but Jane too. I never felt as close as I do now, we are so strong.

Jane: We are our own support network now, that's the thing. If there is any good that can come out of this, then that is definitely one thing. Matt has definitely changed his priorities. Matt thrived on work for a long time, it was a real passion of his. Indirectly, yes, it was supporting the family, but he did it to prove himself. Then something like this happens, and priorities all change around.

For me, it's difficult to say. Watching the children grow really gives me hope. All the time they inspire me, and us being able to enjoy that in turn, as a family. I agree that our family unit, us four, has got stronger. It's made us communicate better and we're both very much aware of that.

It really motivates me. It drives me to do the right things for the right reasons and get our priorities in order. Seeing them grow, becoming strong little people in all of this, that is so very hopeful to me. Gavin, we've seen him learn how to deal with it, deal with himself. Yes, it's been difficult, but he's grown in such a sensible way despite it. It will equip him for life. I just hope Philippa will be able to talk more openly about it one day.

Matt: Yes, Philippa has a journey with it still to come. We both feel that very strongly. I know I can't move on until a line is drawn under this, I can't move on through it. I know it's generalising, but usually blokes are the ones to get on with it, and women like to dwell on things. I'm feeling so feminine in all of this because I just can't move on.

JANE & MATT'S STORY

It will end when he dies and is buried in the ground. It has to be. Not having any justice, that is the only justice I have got. If I have to wait 20 years for it, then so be it. The opposite end of hope has been the despair that the police have left us with. There is really no hope there.

When there is so much hurt and disappointment, it is hard to remain hopeful for very long. Jane and Matt come back to the same themes throughout the interviews, and I have tried to capture the cycle of repetition because it is part of their story. I choose this opportunity to ask them about this.

Matt: It goes on every day. Every single day you go over it.

Jane: Both of us do - without telling each other. We do. Things crop up, like seeing my mother, or we see something in the news or on the TV. It all comes back. Actually, I guess, rather, it never goes.

Matt: There are things that do trigger it, yes, but it is always just there. I know it is very unresolved in me because I have these vivid dreams. I have had dreams about the day he is buried. I am certain I'll spit in his grave as he is lowered into the ground. In my dreams people are standing around the graveside mourning, and I say,

"Actually, I'm glad he's gone, and it's because he's a paedophile, and you lot haven't known a thing about it because *she* didn't tell you. She has not told you the truth about him, and she's treated you badly by not telling you the truth."

My heart tells me that there is all this unresolved stuff in me, through my dreams, and it can be a battle with my head. Most of the time I can control how I want to act, but sometimes the anger builds and builds. This is why there's still a part of me that wants to really hurt him, and unfortunately the longer there is no justice, the more it builds. I have to get on top of it, I really do. I need to get back to the gym - I haven't worked out in a couple of months, and it's all boiling away. It bubbles away. I never experienced anger, true anger, until all of this. I really don't like it. It's really very scary. I'm terrified of one day just flipping. I want to remain in control of myself. It terrifies me.

JANE & MATT'S STORY

I remember the horror on the faces of your mum and sister when I used the word 'paedophile' to describe your dad. They were completely shocked. Well, check the definition in the dictionary. Now, if there's anything on TV about paedophiles I have to watch it. I don't want to; it sickens me, but I just have to. I really need to know why he did it.

Jane: It's trying to make sense of it, trying to understand it.

Matt: I can watch everything there is and I'm still none the wiser. It's insane. This is why I really want the truth from him.

Jane: He probably doesn't know why he did it. I don't think he has the answers, I'm sure of it. Is there a why? He states he doesn't know why he did it, very matter of factly. I don't think he'll try to understand it. Won't accept it.

Where is it in the psychological make-up of someone? Isn't there any way of finding out where it stems from? What is it that triggers someone to do those actions? That's what I'm trying to understand. I really don't understand that if you've been abused and traumatised by

333

someone, why would you want to do it to someone else? Why would you want to hurt someone else? This is my father I'm also talking about. It's very surreal though, even though I've come to terms with it. It feels so surreal. I don't suppose you feel the same, Matt, though?

Matt: Unfortunately, I feel it's all too real. Finding his door and spraying "PAEDO" on it. I so, so desperately want to do this, because that way I can let society mete out justice. Bring his crimes into the open. If they've had to move three or four times, would Jane's mum still be with him? I don't think she can really see the gravity in what he's done. It doesn't help how leniently he was treated by the law, it's colluded with him somehow.

You start imagining the worst things. Who else has he abused? It is haunting. I can't believe for a moment that it was just Jane's sister and our daughter. I think he had it planned, that he knew exactly what he was going to say if he ever got caught. "I was abused..." I'm sure this was in his mind the first time he did it some 30 years ago. He knew exactly what he was going to say, he's very calculating.

Jane: Oh yes, I don't doubt that. He knew what he needed to say. We will never know the truth, and when you do start thinking about it you try not to. Not because you're in denial, but your imagination fills in the gaps a million times, and that's horrendous. You have to try not to think about it, because it's incredibly destructive.

The thing that upsets me the most, that I really despise and hate, and it's not a word we use lightly, but I really hate the way we've been put in this position. That's what upsets me. Not just the physical act that has happened to my child and my sister. We shouldn't have to deal with this. These are our children who are dealing with it. They should be living innocent childhoods and not even have to know about this until they're adults. Then they can deal with it because they've got some kind of life experience. It upsets me a lot. It is a hideous legacy, but you do eventually start to recover.

Matt: There is no doubting that you have to feel worse to feel better. Even telling our story, it's hard, because it reopens the wounds and all the hurt surfaces. You have to do it, so that the wounds heal better. You really have to do it, but you do mend and you do begin to heal. Even in all of this darkness, there is always hope.

JANE & MATT'S STORY

There is so much that remains unresolved for them, and yet when I left their house for the last time, I felt such warmth and confidence that they would both be able to steer their family, and each other, towards recovery.

When Jane and Matt were reviewing the drafts of their story, Matt asked if he had mentioned the word 'hate'. I told him that Jane had mentioned it, but he had not. Matt sent me the words that follow, which I have included as a postscript to their story.

MATT'S POSTSCRIPT:

HOW THE WORD 'HATE' HAS CHANGED MY LIFE

hate:

verb: feel intense dislike for, or a strong aversion towards.
noun: **1** intense dislike; strong aversion. **2** *informal* a disliked person or thing. **3** before a *noun* denoting hostile actions motivated by intense dislike or prejudice: a hate campaign.

I'm sure like many others I had always used the word *'hate'* freely and easily when speaking in everyday situations, with no kind of real understanding of just how it feels to truly hate someone or something. Hate and anger combine to create a truly terrifying combination and it comes with a great deal of misunderstanding.

Having read our story I felt I should clarify a few things so that you too can seriously consider when to use the word, *'hate'*, if ever, again.

I had never really thought of the word 'hate' as being particularly strong before this period in our lives. Expressions such as "I hate vegetables," or "'I hate traffic jams," or "I hate Johnny so and so..." would be used at the

JANE & MATT'S STORY

drop of a hat. The truth is, I didn't *'hate'* anyone or anything, I merely *'didn't like.'*

Since this episode first came to light I can honestly say that I have not once used the word hate in any other way than which is purely reserved for one person and one person only.... my father-in-law. As a matter of fact, others using the word without what it feels like to really hate someone or something actually seems distasteful to me.

It has to be one of the worst emotions one can feel, and coupled with anger, it is so destructive. My life has been a shadow of my former life. It sounds quite melodramatic, but it's as though I could compare it to BC and AD. We have, BA (Before Abuse) and AA (After Abuse). All the time the hatred never subsides inside of me. It bubbles and festers. I can be doing something quite ordinary, and suddenly drift away into a whole other world where it is perfectly normal to seek revenge and exact your hatred on someone. Even the dictionary definition above doesn't seem nearly strong enough to really describe the feeling. It says nothing about how it consumes your entire being, dictates every single decision you make regarding your family and it eats away at every part of you and your life.

Quite simply, I hope no one reading this ever has to feel true hatred for anyone.

Afterword

AFTERWORD

It is hard to know how to end a book like this. This isn't a set of fairy stories where there are happy endings, and nothing is really very neatly tied up. There is evidence of recovery, healing and, hope but sugar coated the stories are not. You may have many more questions reading the stories than have been answered. It may leave you feeling unsettled and lost. This is the reality for those living it too, and it is a kind of parallel process of the whole nightmare.

I hope the stories bring you, the reader, closer to the reality that the sexual abuse of our children is taking place; there really is hurt going on. Each of the stories shows a different struggle but they are all different people, and all will handle things differently. They are united by a common, tragic, story and the unwavering love for their children.

I want to acknowledge each of the contributors again, for reliving the deep hurt of their stories, so that others reading them can benefit from their experiences.

When I met each of the contributors, I asked them why they might have reached for *Hurt,* and what they hoped to have gained from reading it. This is what they said to me.

Kelly would want to believe that there would be hope, when at times she was struggling to believe there was anything but pain and despair. She would want to see that there would be 'light at the end of the tunnel' just as her sister told her.

Asta told me that she would want to believe that it does not mean the end of the world. She would want to find strength that she could get through it, and see how someone else has made it. She would want to believe that there is a better place waiting for her and Freddy at the end of all the hurt, and that one day they would laugh again.

Lauren would want to know how someone dealing with this would be feeling, blow by blow. She would want to read about some of the worst feelings, so that she might be able to accept them in herself more. She would want to believe that she was not going mad. She would want to know how others coped with this whole situation, where society makes you feel worse than you already do. She would want to feel that there were friends out there, to relieve her from such an isolating experience.

Matt told me that he would hope that he would not feel so alone. He would also want to see a pathway of what might happen – particularly when coming up against the system. He would want to see how someone has dealt with it before him.

Jane would read this book to help her make sense of her own experience. She would be desperate to read how

AFTERWORD

someone else had coped, so that she had something to compare herself with: someone to help her face up to some of the tough issues and decisions. She would want someone's story to help her not feel so isolated.

Have I done them justice? I hope I have.

WHERE TO GO
FOR HELP

WHERE TO GO FOR HELP

If you are worried about the safety of a child, and want to find out what you might do:

http://www.nspcc.org.uk/

Call NSPCC helpline on **0808 800 5000**

If you are worried about someone you know, whom you think might be harming a child:

http://www.stopitnow.org.uk/

Call Stop it Now on **0808 1000 900**

If you are a non-abusing parent or carer of a child who has been sexually abused:

http://www.mosac.org.uk/

Call Mosac on **0800 980 1958**

If you were sexually abused in childhood, and you are looking for support:

http://www.napac.org.uk/

Call NAPAC on **0800 085 3330**

lıp

ATTENTION WRITERS

Do you want to get published?

LIP works with Authors in the fields of self-help, health, healing, mind body & spirit and personal development.

We want to help you turn your creative work into a reality.

We make publishing fast, easy and fun! And we help you live the dream by getting your books, e-books, CDs and MP3s published and distributed across a global network.

For more information visit our website at:

www.liveitpublishing.com

LIP... The easiest way to get published!

Lightning Source UK Ltd.
Milton Keynes UK
UKOW032346100513

210521UK00005B/49/P